ESCAPE FROM SCEPTICISM
Liberal Education as if Truth Mattered

ESCAPE FROM SCEPTICISM
Liberal Education as if Truth Mattered

CHRISTOPHER DERRICK

Sherwood Sugden & Company
PUBLISHERS

1117 Eighth Street, La Salle, Illinois 61301

ISBN 0-89385-002-9

Copyright © 1977 by Christopher Derrick.

All rights reserved. No part of this book may be reproduced or transmitted in any form or by any means, electronic or mechanical, including photocopying, recording, or by any information storage and retrieval system (excepting short passages for purposes of review), without permission in writing from the publisher.

Copies of this book may be had by writing to:

Sherwood Sugden & Company, Publishers
1117 Eighth Street
La Salle, Illinois 61301

and enclosing a check or money order for:

1 copy: $1.95 plus 50 cents handling and postage
2, 3, or 4 copies: $1.95 each plus 25 cents per book, handling and postage
5 or more copies: $1.50 each plus 20 cents per book, handling and postage

(Illinois residents please add 5 percent sales tax. Prices subject to change without notice.)

Printed in the United States of America.

CONTENTS

I. THE STUDENT PREDICAMENT — 1

II. EDUCATION FOR FREEDOM — 11

III. IN THE SUPERMARKET — 23

IV. SCEPTICISM AND THE ACADEMIC — 35

V. PIGS IS PIGS — 47

VI. WHO CLAIMS TO KNOW? — 59

VII. THE WORD 'CATHOLIC' — 73

VIII. THE SEVENFOLD WAY — 89

IX. DREAM AND REALITY — 103

*To Dr. Ronald P. McArthur
and the students and faculty of
Thomas Aquinas College
Calabasas, California*

AUTHOR'S NOTE

I must apologize to a wise friend and mentor for taking his subtitle without permission and adapting it to my own use.

By way of reparation, I would like to give him a free advertisement. To anyone interested in the subject of this book I therefore recommend *Small Is Beautiful: Economics as if People Mattered*, by E.F. Schumacher, Part II, Chapter 1.

—C.H.D.

Chapter I:
THE STUDENT PREDICAMENT

In the chill misty morning, I sit down here by the lakeside. The water is entirely calm, and reflects the shape of that low bridge to perfection.

How pleasant it is that the good plain-faced ducks should come feathering and quacking around me! I love ducks, I identify with them: I couldn't possibly think of eating them. Now, on this quiet Californian morning, I amuse myself by choosing romantic names for the individual ducks which are my present company: Florestan, Eusebius, Sophonisba. In a perplexed and baffling world, there's something reassuring about the reality, the clear-cut objectivity of their existence. You can trust a duck.

But even in this beautiful place, even in this agreeable company, the uncertainties of a despairing time can sometimes come flooding back to terrify the mind. Are these ducks *really* real and trustworthy? Is anything real? Is there such a thing as 'truth' or 'reality' at all? And if there is, can we lay hold of it? Or are we doomed to a life of radical scepticism, of perpetual uncertainty?

Perhaps I should put such thoughts out of my mind, by brute force if necessary. "That way madness lies".

But they do make some kind of possibly dangerous claim upon our attention, and not only because respected philosophers talk about them: we have all been asking such questions since early childhood, and not only with the more lunatic side of our minds. Somebody once defined philosophy as the subject which children ask questions about, until their exasperated parents tell them not to be so silly. It isn't an entirely bad definition. Mummy, where has yesterday gone? Mummy, why is it *me* who's 'me'? Mummy, are dreams real?

Escape from Scepticism

Is reality a dream? Is 'truth' true? And does it *matter*?

These are big questions, and many people would answer them sceptically. Not far away, on other campuses, there are extremely learned philosophers who would cast serious doubts upon my beloved ducks. What *is* a duck, after all? Does it exist, does it *be*, or is it just one momentary appearance within an endless flux of becoming? Is it perhaps something which I invent for reasons unknown to my concious mind, a tribally-conditioned construct from unreliable sense-data? Or is it perhaps real, but so existentially unique that I shouldn't really see it (as I must in fact) as one duck among other ducks? Will I need to discover or invent some kind of universal Duckhood, an ideal *enteheit* which stands enthroned forever in some Platonic heaven, imperfectly embodied in each of the feathered shapes before me?

It's all very perplexing, and we shouldn't really blame the philosophers for interfering with the common-sense ordinariness of things, as though this were giving no trouble until they intruded upon it. All men find reality perplexing: the philosophers put this perplexity into words, and usefully. It's when they try to resolve the problem with nihilistic or absurd answers—that's when they start to worry me.

I look up now, past a rounded tree which quivers with bird-life, and I see a few of the students. Once again, it's a kind of shock to gaze upon them. They aren't in the least like the current image or stereotype of what students ought to be: they fail most lamentably to come up to my expectations. For one thing, they are quietly dressed and soberly behaved, though nearly always cheerful and sometimes—in the best sense—rowdy: for another, they display a most unorthodox kind of dedication and hope, a firm belief in the value of what they're doing at this college. This isn't because they suppose themselves to have found an easy and certain road to 'success' of the economic and social kind: their studies here are arduous, and have only the most tenuous relationship to the acquisition of any marketable skills. Their confidence is of a different kind. In the group which I'm now watching, I recognize one or two with whom I was talking far into the wee hours last night; and what I remember is their deep trust in reality and in reason, their conviction that the human mind can actually apprehend truth and that the effort involved in this exercise is amply worthwhile.

'Reality', 'truth': on many a campus, these corny old words would provoke an ironically sceptical raising of eyebrows. But not here.

And these students aren't on their way to burn the library or otherwise to 'protest', according to a fashion that was recently dominant and still retains much power: they're on their way to Mass, though under no kind of compulsion. And believe it or not, the Mass is going to be mostly in Latin, and in full obedience to the discipline of distant and un-American Rome: worse still, these children actually *know* Latin, and can take part in the Church's worship in the language of the Western and Christian centuries. They are growing up, easily and naturally, into some larger citizenship than that of California. What kind of a freaked-out world have I wandered into?

Florestan and Eusebius and Sophonisba are splashing around very happily, causing the reflected image of the bridge to tremble. These ducks don't appear to be in any doubt as to their own real existence. Their wisdom might be greater than that of the academies.

It might be no bad thing if I got up and joined those deviationist students at Mass.

What am I doing on this campus? Why should a middle-aged Englishman—a literary critic by profession, self-indulgent in his personal habits, somewhat inclined therefore to insolvency and stoutness—why should such a man find himself six-and-a-half thousand miles from home, sitting by a Californian lakeside, and marvelling at certain students whose backgrounds and whose personal preoccupations and problems are six-and-a-half million miles from his own?

What kind of a world have I wandered into, and why?

Mass is over, though a good many of the students have remained in the chapel for further devotions of their own. I walk out slowly, full of the Sacrament, my ears ringing with archaic words that go back to the roots of our civilization.

Our civilization? What is that, and where does it stand? Do we actually possess such a thing? And if so, is it in any fit state to be handed on to the next generation? And *how*?

Thorny questions for a perplexed world. I am here because on a previous and rather brief visit, I thought I detected some hint of an answer to them. To put it more cautiously, I thought that these particular students would serve as a hang-peg or starting-point for a prolonged worry and meditation that might possibly get somewhere. Their condition, their enterprise suggested that the whole idea of 'liberal education' might need re-thinking. Various questions of the philosophical kind would then arise, various questions of the religious kind as well. Some of them might even be answerable.

I feel drawn to such an enquiry, though somewhat frightened of it as well. Presumably my motives ought to be purely intellectual, governed only by a passion for truth, which does indeed matter: although no philosopher, I do possess an intellect of sorts. But I'm also a parent, worried at a very earthy and practical level about the problem of education, the problem of what one generation can usefully and lovingly pass on to the next, and how. One loves one's own dear children so very much! What can one give them that's going to be useful, in so very ominous a future?

> "The windows of the world are blurred with tears,
> And troubles come like cloud-banks from the west"

—how can one offer them honest comfort? What assurances can we give them, at a time when many of our finest brains would cast doubt even upon the knowable existence of a duck—when the universities, which surely ought to be the guiding lights of our society and the focal points of its wisdom, seem rather to be centers of scepticism and despair and disaffection?

This college lacks that kind of character, at all events. I have visited many colleges and universities and been deeply involved with several, in the United States and elsewhere: here, what struck me first was the exceptional happiness of the students.

I can't help considering such matters—first of all—from a parent's point of view, and in a mood of habitual anxiety about the fragile happiness of the young. They are so much more vulnerable than they suppose!

One can always forget this, of course, and entertain comforting fantasies about the total bliss of being a young adult, a student especially.

> "The Freshman ambles down the High,
> In love with everything he sees,
> He notes the racing autumn sky,
> He sniffs a lively autumn breeze"

—shouldn't he be lyrically, ideally happy? He is carefree, after all, without external responsibilities; he is privileged in some degree; he is engaged in studies that ought to be fascinating; he has the world at his feet: above all, he is *young*. But honest memory will tell us that it was never quite as golden as that, even in our own long-distant day: youth can be a kind of hell, and the suicide-rate at the universities was always distinctly high. One never assured the immediate happiness of one's son by packing him off to college.

And when all allowance is made for false perspective and selective reporting, it seems undeniable that the university scene has been marked—during the last twenty years or so—by a rather exceptional degree of stress and bitterness. College is an unhappier place than it used to be: it gives more cause for that distinctively parental kind of anxiety.

One must not get this matter out of proportion. During the 1960s, some people talked as though 'student unrest' and 'campus disorder' were new and astonishing phenomena. This was unrealistic. The young—and perhaps especially the *clever* young—have always been somewhat riotous, somewhat ill-behaved from time to time, somewhat loud and pharisaical in their criticism of their elders' world and conduct. At the best, this has been sound and useful criticism: at the worst, the young have behaved as we must expect fallen human nature to behave, at an age when physical and intellectual energies are high, but seldom governed by any wide experience of the human condition and of its limitations.

If the modern student tends to break out, denounce, and rampage, he is behaving in a highly traditional manner: he is following precedents that were established long ago, in thirteenth-century Bologna, in the Paris of Thomas Aquinas and later of Ignatius Loyola, and in mediaeval Oxford's bloody confrontations of Town and Gown.

Granted so much, there does seem to be a new bitterness nowadays, a new despair: on the average English or American campus today, students appear to be under exceptional pressure, of a kind which impels some towards drugs and the narcotic use of sex, some towards petty violence, some towards revolutionary extremism, some towards dull acquiescence in a mindless Babbittism, and too many towards suicide. Even in my own university—Oxford, "towery city and branchy between towers"—the new and furious kind of 'student' seems to have taken over from the older-style 'undergraduate', with his tweeds and his huge pipe and his reading-parties in the Black Forest and his possible wild bonneting of a bobby on Boat-Race night. The towers remain, even many of the branches; but the Oxford of sacred and perhaps sentimental memory—the Oxford of Newman, of *Sinister Street* and *Brideshead Revisited*—has vanished, "submerged now and obliterated, irrecoverable as Lyonesse, so quickly have the waters come flooding in". Even among all that mellow old stonework and those still-chiming bells, the spirit of barbarian bitterness appears to have taken over to a sad degree: it's a universal phenomenon, or getting on that way.

To some extent, of course, it's a phenomenon of twentieth-century culture in general, and not merely of the universities and colleges; and if its on-campus version has been particularly noticeable in recent years, there may have been particular reasons for this. One can point, for example, at the enormous size of too many present-day universities and their consequent impersonality, especially in the United States. The young man leaves school full of fine ideas, and with a powerful sense of his own centrality in the universe: he sees himself as approaching a fountain of learning and wisdom, he dreams (perhaps) of intimate membership in an adult academic community, and he may already know the names of the world-famous scholars and scientists who are its elder statesmen and its prime adornments. But too often he finds himself a very small frog in an absurdly large pool, jostled and elbowed aside by a million other frogs, taught (in practice) by graduate instructors of very junior status, and only meeting those great minds on the most occasional and distant kind of basis.

He is likely to suffer a threefold shock. Its first impact is social: he makes that discovery that the university is a crowd rather than a community. Its second impact is educational: he is offered an enormous multiplicity of academic choices, but with very little suggestion as to how they can be related to one another, or to the problems of the student and his world. And its third impact is philosophical. He was full of outward swagger and assurance when he came to the university: he was, after all, a very young man. But the immense age and dignity and prestige of the academic institution was present to his mind, perhaps not consciously: he was expecting wisdom, he was expecting the answers. Now, he discovers that his elders don't really claim to know their way round the universe any better than he did as a child. The best wisdom that the university can teach him is that there is no wisdom.

If, in this situation, he turns riotous and nihilistic, I'm entirely on his side: that is to say, if the universe actually had the character attributed to it by the dominant scepticism of the day, if there were no such things as ascertainable truth and objective value, if human beings had no particular nature or destiny beyond what they could invent for themselves, then it would be entirely rational to respond to such a universe in a spirit of anarchic defiance, and to behave accordingly on campus. Not all students ever went as far as that: the tumults of the 1960s were over-reported in the media, and at the time of writing, they seem to have settled down considerably. Even so, it is hardly surprising if the present-day student starts to doubt the value of the whole educational and academic exercise, its ends no less than its immediately bewildering means. He knows, however vaguely, that he is here to undergo a kind of long initiation, a graduation into fully adult society. But in some respects, his situation is less fortunate than that of his tribal and 'primitive' forefathers. Is there in fact a coherent adult society which he can respect, so that graduation into it can become his sufficient objective? And while the older generation can teach him techniques and particulars very efficiently, can they give him anything like an accepted and plausible tribal wisdom? Apart from the numerous and unrelated kinds of *expertise* associated with their various fields, is there any real sense in which these countless faculty-members know what they're doing?

The student is hardly to be blamed if he answers such questions negatively, or sceptically at least—if he comes to see his college education in distinctly cynical terms, as a means to self-advancement and no more, a way of getting some better-paid job, and never mind all that fancy talk about what an ideally 'liberal' education ought to be. He may even come to see the whole vast education-industry as a kind of racket or hoax, or perhaps as an idol or sacred cow. Speaking personally, I myself have often suspected that 'education' is one of the great false gods worshipped—*faute de mieux*—by our otherwise godless society: countless people talk as though there were some kind of automatic and mystical value in the mere fact of being in a lecture-room, lectured by somebody about something for some purpose. In the abstract, knowledge is of course better than ignorance. But in any concrete case, I would want to know a great deal more before agreeing that this situation and experience was indeed desirable. It frequently is; but it's sometimes a complete waste of time, and it's occasionally a great deal worse. The great god Education could do with a certain amount of criticism and challenge: he seems to command rather more allegiance than he deserves.

As things now stand, he does command it; and thus there arises a sharp clash and contradiction between the student's own desires and the purposes which the college or university would claim—in its loftier moments—to serve. Who is to be blamed for this? It's easy enough to blame the student: he is obviously in a somewhat false position if, while not desiring the distinctive commodity offered by higher education, he none the less feels constrained to go through the motions of buying. This falsity is hardly his fault, however: it's partly the fault of parents and teachers, and partly the fault of society at large—especially of those potential employers who, in their laziness, demand degrees because they cannot be bothered to evaluate the individuals before them. Sometimes we can blame politics. Here in the United States, for example, 'student unrest' was at its highest—or at least received most publicity—at the time of maximum involvement in the Viet-Nam war. Only an extreme cynic would deny that much of the student protest against that war had moral and idealistic motivations. But at the same time, only an extreme innocent will see no connection at all between the fact of student exemption from the draft and the presence on campus of so many young men who seemed indifferent or hostile to everything that a university can conceivably be or do or offer.

But this is only one extreme instance of a wider phenomenon. All over the world, young people are entering universities and colleges for reasons which have little to do with any pure vocation to higher studies. They become students almost reluctantly—under pressure from teachers and parents, or in order to qualify for that better-paid job, or simply as a way of deferring the great problem of what to do with life while retaining the freedom and irresponsibility of childhood for a few years longer. Supply and demand are painfully ill-related: even where the university bends over backwards to sell what such young people want, or suppose themselves to want, a considerable amount of stress is inevitable, and bitterness by reason of it.

I had seen that stress and bitterness in many places: its absence was what struck me first when I came to this rather unusual campus in California. Here, I thought—and initially, with the merely parental and compassionate part of my mind—is something which needs looking into.

What makes these particular students so conspicuously different? What is the basis of their happiness, their confidence, and (perhaps above all) their hope? It can't be any assurance of worldly success: the times are uncertain for all, most of them are far from rich, and the kind of education which they're getting here is—by the narrow standards of mere vocational and financial ambition—a shade preposterous. Their friends at home tell them so. Philosophy? *Theology?* Are you going to be a priest (or nun)? No? Then what *use* is it? Are you crazy?

Some of them (to my certain knowledge) would reply that this kind of education helps them to become free men and women in a society of slaves.

What a silly arrogant way of talking! They live in a free country, slavery is a thing of the past.

Wait: be patient. There could be a real question here. Let us sit and talk it over, down here by the lakeside, while those crazy students grapple with Aristotle and Aquinas in the classrooms nearby.

Chapter II:
EDUCATION FOR FREEDOM

In this book, I want to undertake a meditative re-examination of what 'liberal education' ought to mean and be, against a background of certain more fundamental questions, and mostly in connection with the 'liberal arts college' as found in the United States.

When undertaken by anybody with my particular bias, such a task has to begin with semantics, with some consideration of what is *meant* by that adjective 'liberal'. On the face of it, this might seem a fairly simple subject. When used in political and economic contexts, it is a word of more or less clear and agreed meaning—though since Englishmen use it in one sense and Americans in a subtly different sense, it can generate transatlantic misunderstandings and cross-purposes. And when we change the subject and start talking about the 'liberal arts' or 'liberal education', we shall be giving the adjective a sharply different meaning but one which is still clear and agreed: we shall be discussing a broadly 'cultural' field of activity and study, lying between the fine arts on the one hand and the sciences and technologies on the other.

Between these two meanings of the word, the semantic cleavage is now complete. When used in England, the phrase 'a liberal education' does not carry even the faintest suggestion of an education in the principles (whatever they may be) of the Liberal Party: any such interpretation of it would seem like a pun, and a bad one. And I once heard an American expressing his concern at the growth of 'liberalism' in his country, and proposing a revivified 'liberal education' as the best means of resisting this undesirable trend. The apparent contradiction had escaped his notice altogether: for all practical purposes, 'liberal' is now two separate and unrelated words.

But its use in connection with education is clear and unambiguous. If a man has enjoyed the blessing of a good liberal education, we feel, he will not be directly qualified thereby to follow any particular profession. On the other hand, he will have been encouraged to develop himself more fully as a man. He will be well-read, informed, sensitive; he will have some appreciation of the fine arts, some understanding of the world and its history and its problems: his sympathies will be broad and his mind will be tolerant, and if there arises some question of the public or political kind, he will bring to the discussion of this something better than mere prejudice and self-interest. He will have some skill in the difficult arts of reading and writing and thinking: he will have inner resources, he'll be worth talking to.

Now if a man has all these admirable characteristics, he will in fact be highly employable: there are many offices, both public and private, which call for no particular and specialized skills in those who hold them, but only for a certain quality of mind and character. In this sense, it can be economically advantageous to acquire a liberal education, as defined and certified by a college degree: it will get you a better job. But to think on these lines, except in a minor and marginal kind of way, is to court self-contradiction. The very idea of liberal education, at its best, presupposes at least a temporary abandonment of all such concerns. Such an education puts before you a range of studies and activities which are considered to be worth undertaking for their own sake, and likely to be spoiled or corrupted if undertaken for any ulterior motive: it proposes to make you into a certain definable kind of man, not for social and economic advantage, but because of an underlying belief that it's inherently desirable to be a man of that specific kind.

In an imperfect world, one can hardly expect an ideal of this sort to be achieved very completely or very extensively. Life is insecure, society is competitive, the freedom of the young is overshadowed by the problem of earning a living: neither among students nor among their teachers will it be easy to find such completely pure and disinterested motivations. But at least we can see here an ideal, one to which individuals and institutions can approximate in some measure; and it is an ideal which has been pursued and loved and developed by many outstanding people over a long period.

But it is an ideal which—in our time—has run into serious difficulties: I hinted at some aspects of these in the previous chapter. Its great weakness is that it presupposes a general consensus about human values, a general agreement about what kind of man or woman one would ideally wish to be; and while we know from history that such a consensus or agreement *can* exist over wide areas and for long periods, we also know from experience that nothing of the sort exists in our present society. We are sharply divided about human values: different groups entertain radically different notions about the kind of man or woman one would ideally wish to be, while others deny the possibility of any such ideal, saying that it doesn't matter in the least.

One might therefore conclude that in a society so divided and pluralistic, liberal education can have no coherence or direction and must therefore be a lost cause. In my view, this would be altogether too pessimistic a conclusion. But the concept does at least need re-examination; and we can usefully begin this by asking *why* we apply the word 'liberal' to a certain kind of education, or to a certain ideal of what education might possibly be and do. We all know that this word has something to do with the complex idea of 'freedom'; and most of us know that if we go far enough back in history and semantics, the *liberalis* is the free man as distinct from the *servus* or slave. Historically speaking, a 'liberal education' ought to be the kind of education that's considered suitable for a free man and relevant to his activities and preoccupations, as against the lower or 'servile' kind of instruction which is deemed sufficient for the slave.

Such an understanding of the word might be considered obsolete, of no relevance to present-day situations. Slavery—in the full sense of the word—exists no longer except in certain backward corners of the world: in practically every society that we know, the Communist societies included, it is impossible for anyone to hold property-rights over the person of another man.

None the less, I suggest that there are at least two senses in which the distant memory of that 'peculiar institution' remains active in our minds, governing our use of the word 'liberal', especially when we apply it to education: somewhere in the submerged depths of our consciousness, we still regard certain kinds of mentality and certain kinds of activity as distinctively servile.

I regard this as a broadly realistic way of thinking, relevant also to the problems of our colleges; and I would like to analyse it a little.

This is somewhat delicate ground: it sounds rather elitist and snobbish, it sounds like a sneer at the unfortunate and oppressed, to say that certain people have servile mentalities. But this is only a particular and frankly-expressed statement of something which all of us know, and which is taken for granted by practically all parenthood, education, custom, law, and religion—namely, that it isn't a matter of indifference what sort of person you are; that it's much more desirable to be *this* sort of person than to be *that* sort of person. There are indeed some who deny the propriety and even the possibility of making such value-judgments; but they are few in number, and they seldom press home the full logic of their anarchistic position. (Education, they will tell you, must in no sense *guide* the young man: it must merely give him the widest possible scope for 'doing his own thing'. But what if the 'thing' in question turns out to be murderous, on Nazi or otherwise racial lines, as it sometimes will?)

For most of us, it is a fact of experience and common-sense that education has to be governed by *some* set of human values, however sharply we may disagree about the content of these. We regard it as desirable to grow up as *this* sort of person, within a wide range of particular possibilities, and we therefore can't help regarding it as a misfortune or even a disaster to grow up as *that* sort of person. But we should be able to discuss such questions calmly and charitably: the evils of snobbery and elitism only arise when this whole subject is made into a pretext for pride and contempt.

I regard it as a misfortune or even a disaster to have a servile mentality. By this, I do not necessarily mean any kind of mentality that we might find among actual slaves: it was recognized as early as Aristotle's time that where slavery exists, the servile mentality does not always coincide with servile status. Nor am I using this adjective in its modern sense, to suggest a mentality of the fawning, abject, sycophantic kind. If I say that a man has a servile mentality, I mean that his thoughts and responses are narrow, small, petty, ignoble, and mean. He may be intelligent, or sharp and clever at least; but he lacks magnanimity, he is incapable of high thoughts and generous emotions, and he takes better men than himself to be fools when they display such thoughts and such emotions.

When a man has this kind of mentality, it may be partly his own fault and partly the fault of his inheritance and family environment. But it seems to me clear that certain types of education foster this servility of the mind, and that any liberal education which deserves the name will work hard—and, let us hope, successfully—in the opposite sense.

If you and I had acquaintances in common, I could probably illustrate this depressing phenomenon by whispering a few names in your ear. As things are, I can best illustrate it from fiction; and as an English writer addressing a chiefly American readership, I had better choose English novels for the purpose.

Two examples spring to mind. The first is an academic sociologist called Mark Studdock, in C.S. Lewis's novel *That Hideous Strength*. He has the servile mentality indeed. "It must be remembered that in Mark's mind hardly one rag of noble thought, either Christian or pagan, had a secure lodging. His education had been neither scientific nor classical—merely 'Modern'. The severities both of abstraction and of high human tradition had passed him by; and he had neither peasant shrewdness nor aristocratic honour to help him. He was a man of straw, a glib examinee in subjects that require no exact knowledge (he had always done well on Essays and General Papers). . . ."

My second example is a young officer called Hooper, in Evelyn Waugh's *Brideshead Revisited*. "Hooper had no illusions about the Army—or rather no special illusions distinguishable from the general, enveloping fog from which he observed the universe. . . . Hooper was no romantic. He had not as a child ridden with Rupert's horse or sat among the camp-fires at Xanthus-side; at the age when my eyes were dry to all save poetry—that stoic, redskin interlude which our schools introduce between the fast-flowing tears of the child and the man—Hooper had wept often, but never for Henry's speech on St Crispin's day, nor for the epitaph at Thermopylae. The history they taught him had few battles in it but, instead, a profusion of detail about humane legislation and recent industrial change."

In each of these character-sketches—they deserve full study in context—one can recognise the same sad type, familiar to most of us from social experience. No question of class-snobbery is even implied. Hooper is a commissioned officer, and plainly has a big future in business before him if he survives the war: Studdock is a distinctly successful academic, recently accepted (when the story begins) into the powerful 'inner ring' or elite-group of his college. Both novelists portrayed far humbler characters in very much more favourable terms. The thing blamed in either case, explicitly and precisely, is a type of education and the type of mind it produces. One might call this the Gross National Product: I call it the servile mentality.

One characteristic of this mentality is that it evaluates all things in terms of immediate economic or practical advantage. In order to see this tendency in action, I suggest that you seek out that person of your acquaintance who most closely resembles Studdock and Hooper, and start talking to him about the value of Latin in education. Quite infallibly, he will say: "But what *use* is it?"

That question can in fact be answered quite sufficiently at its own level. But it would be more appropriate—though perhaps less prudent—for you to reply: "You wouldn't say that if you didn't have the mind of a slave".

This brings me to the second and more important of my two senses in which the concept of slavery is relevant to present-day education. Some minds are servile; but then, so are some activities. The slave works because he must, and to serve purposes which are not his own. And in the same way, most of us (in our working hours) do things which have got to be done, in order to serve purposes which are distinct from themselves. The part of our education which teaches us how to do these things can rightly be called servile. Liberal education is something else: it teaches us how to do things which are not 'necessary'—not dictated by considerations of the practical or economic kind—but are worth doing for their own sake.

In order to make this crucial distinction, Aristotle used a bold analogy. The free man, he said, is the man who lives for his own sake and not (like the slave) for others; and in the same way, philosophy is the most 'free' of all subjects and studies, because it is undertaken solely for its own sake and is—as that man with a slave-mentality would say—entirely 'useless'. This analogy (it was almost a pun) played a crucial part in the long process of semantic development which eventually caused us to regard 'liberal' as a suitable word for certain studies, certain types of education.

Perhaps unfortunately or perhaps not, most of us nowadays are only 'free' in our few hours of leisure and holiday. For the most part, our time is taken up with servile work; and if that seems an unsuitable adjective for our interesting jobs and our noble professions, this may be because selective memory causes us to associate slavery too simply with low status and menial tasks and perhaps with membership in some subject race. It may be as well to remember that in quite a number of societies, it has been possible for a man to achieve great wealth and power, and even to control the political destinies of his nation, while still remaining legally a slave. This word should not be associated too simply with menial activities.

To think of 'liberal education', therefore, is to think of studies and activities which are worth undertaking for their own sake, and not only or chiefly because of the accidental advantages which they can sometimes bring us.

But this understanding of the phrase, though straightforward and plausible on the surface, raises some embarrassing questions when we start to consider it in depth. It takes us away from the agreed and manageable world of means and into the uncertain and disputed world of ends; and we may find this transition painful, just as an actual slave can be disoriented and made miserable by sudden liberation.

Our society is extremely good at means. If there's some definable task which has to be done for reasons lying outside itself—if there's a bridge to be built, or a patient to be healed, or a man to be put on the moon—more skill will now be deployed, and with far better hope of success, than at any time in the past. We are clever at such tasks, clever also at the business of training men to perform them: servile education knows what it's doing, and is in good shape generally.

But our pluralistic and divided society has no corresponding agreement and assurance about ends, about ultimate values: our liberal education therefore does not and cannot know what it's doing, and is in bad shape generally.

Our illustration of this sad fact is provided by a phenomenon which was often reported—from different countries—during the student protests and upheavals of the 1960s. There was a high degree of correlation between the subjects chiefly studied and the intensity of expressed bitterness and stress. Your furious loud protestor was typically a student of the humanities or the social sciences—very often, of sociology in particular: seldom indeed was he a student of engineering or medicine.

This makes sense: it could have been predicted. The engineer and the doctor serve purposes which are secondary or 'servile', but which are clearly understood and can in fact be achieved: from the college level onwards, their studies and activities have the psychologically rewarding character of being manageable, and therefore promote a certain relaxation of the mind. But the more liberal kind of education, when undertaken in a society as divided and sceptical about ultimate values as ours is, must be expected to have the opposite effect—to be unsettling, to engender stress. The literary student can perhaps retreat into mere aestheticism, but the sociologist is bound to be in trouble: he is expected to concern himself with the study and management of human society, in the total absence of any consensus about what human beings are and what values should govern their social life. He is bound to experience stress and frustration; and if he works this off in protest and violence, we should not really be surprised.

This is a real problem, and it's seldom faced squarely. It's all very well to talk glibly about studies and activities which are worth undertaking 'for their own sake'. But what studies and activities are those? How do we know? Who decides? Does the student choose for himself? And what kind of 'sake' is involved anyway? It's all very well to speak of turning from means to ends. But what are the 'ends' of human existence? The idea of liberal education presumes that we have cleared the ground and overcome immediate practical problems, however briefly, and are therefore free to pursue our destiny as human beings. But in that very presumption, it brings us face to face with the thorny problem of what that destiny might be—the problem (to put it brutally) of what human life is *for*. And for our pluralist and sceptical society as a whole, this is an unanswered and perhaps unanswerable question, a very painful question therefore.

Its painfulness will not always be present and recognized in the conscious mind. There is a crude sense in which we can say that the problem of liberal education is the problem of education for leisure; and most of us, whether liberally educated or not, find it possible to cope with this latter problem in some fairly satisfactory way without raising too many awkward questions. Close family life and the pleasures and burdens of domesticity will often mean that there's very little genuinely spare time left over to be filled; and if there is some, hobbies and sports and the enjoyable routines of petty sociability can come to our rescue.

Even so, a real problem of leisure does exist over large areas of modern society, and painfully, if we can judge by the efforts made to avoid facing it. Many or most of us retain some memory of the old idea that work is the means and leisure the end; but in the actual experience of many people's lives, this situation comes fairly close to being reversed. Work becomes the interesting, structured, and meaningful part of existence, and leisure becomes something that serves the purposes of work: we use it to rest and relax, to refresh ourselves, and so re-charge our batteries for the next day's servile exertions. At the worst, leisure becomes a kind of meaningless gap that has to be filled somehow; and hence there arises the enormous modern demand for distraction, for non-stop entertainment, so that leisure-time sees the whole family slumped around the television, physically together, but with each one psychologically encapsulated into his own private relationship with the screen and its phantasmal images. Hence also—in some degree—the idea that the mother of a family should be back at work as soon as child-care ceases to take up the whole of her time. The desire for more money is of course relevant here, as is the low esteem in which family life tends to be held today. But there's also a background assumption that the world of work is a world of meaning and fulfillment, as against the spoilt idleness of the 'lady of leisure'.

There is undoubtedly something in this. It makes a good deal of empirical sense to associate leisure with frivolity: aristocrats and wealthy people in general, although splendidly 'free' in every economic and practical sense, have seldom used their freedom in the high-minded and dedicated way proposed by Aristotle in the *Metaphysics*. Some have done so: most have not.

It is widely believed that liberal education can and should resolve this problem of leisure by promoting activities and interests of the artistic, literary, and generally cultural kind—and even, that this is its prime function. People have to earn their livings, they have to acquire marketable skills somehow. But then, by way of compensation and a higher kind of fulfillment, the individual can also be instructed in various cultural activities—in creative activities possibly, and in appreciation at least. Thus, throughout his life, his leisure will become meaningful: he will be a man of inner resources and lofty preoccupations, deeply involved in the inherited culture of the past, the developing culture of the present.

As an answer to the problem of leisure, this is much better than no answer at all: liberal education, when so conceived, has much to commend it. Its great limitation is that it erects culture and the arts into a kind of substitute religion, which was the destiny prophesied by Matthew Arnold for poetry. This has indeed happened, and widely: there are many people for whom culture is the ultimately serious thing, the medium by which the soul is enlightened and a kind of salvation achieved, the thing which you mustn't joke about. But culture and the arts are themselves the first victims of this illusion: it puts upon them a load which they cannot possibly carry, as is made clear by their present shattered condition. It also perpetuates the false nineteenth-century dichotomy between loftily-conceived 'art' and good productive work in *any* field; and it is a terrible promoter of hypocrisy or pretense. A great intensity of aesthetic response is common in adolescence and youth, but much less common thereafter: many adults, from whose real experience "the glory and the dream" has long departed, feel socially and psychologically obliged to pretend that it hasn't, that they are still ploughed up by poems and paintings and plays and the rest, as most of us were in fact ploughed up by such things during the brief personal Renaissance that normally follows upon the completion of puberty. In fact, such things now leave them almost completely cold. But they have to pretend: otherwise, the free or leisured part of their life would lose a great proportion of the meaning which their liberal education proposed for it.

Frank enquiry, among your more candid friends, will make it clear that these generalizations are amply justified.

With all these considerations in mind, I conclude that liberal education is bound to be insufficient and directionless and otherwise in big trouble except where it can presuppose a religion, or at least a philosophy of life, which is plausible and generally agreed. So far as its prospects in present-day Western society are concerned, this is obviously bad news.

But the word 'liberal', as applied to education, has a further meaning which may perhaps be helpful. It can refer not only to the purpose of study and education, but also to the conditions under which these activities are undertaken.

This seems to me a clearly active sense of the word: that is to say, when people talk about 'liberal education' as a desirable thing, they are not only referring to an education *for* freedom. They are also, and perhaps predominantly, referring to an education *by means of* freedom. In this kind of sense, the antithesis of 'liberal' would be something like 'dogmatic' or 'authoritarian': the implication is that if the liberal arts college is to deserve that highly commendatory adjective, it must do so not only by proposing some kind of freedom as its end-product but also by establishing freedom here and now, by conducting its whole academic and intellectual operation—of research and teaching—in an atmosphere of totally unfettered choice. The student must be entirely free to choose whatever subjects and courses may take his fancy: more importantly still, the teacher and researcher must enjoy total freedom of enquiry and of the intellect. Whatever else may happen on campus, there must be nothing like dogmatism or an imposed orthodoxy, and anything like a heresy-hunt would be the worst of all corruptions. The college or university is concerned, after all, with the discovery and dissemination of truth; and it is only through intellectual and academic freedom that we can come to the truth.

This particular dogmatism is, in fact, the accepted orthodoxy of most liberal education today: anyone who challenged it might well become the victim of a heresy-hunt. But I'm bold enough to take the risk; and initially, to suggest that it is not necessarily the *whole* truth to say that freedom brings us to the truth. There was at least one wise man—a sage or prophet, considered divine by his followers—who saw things the other way round, and therefore said: "The truth shall make you free."

What would happen to the idea of liberal education, as seen from the student's side and also from the faculty's side, if we considered it in His kind of perspective?

Chapter III:
IN THE SUPERMARKET

Seldom indeed, in a reasonably wide experience of people and institutions, have I encountered such an atmosphere of freedom as I have found on this particular Californian campus. And this impression of mine is strongly confirmed by what the students tell me—especially those of them who have previously attended other colleges and universities. For them it was a quite startling liberation to come here; and my parental heart is gladdened accordingly.

But I'm not such a complete fool as to suppose that 'freedom' is an entirely simple concept. It isn't: in matters political and social and personal and (I would add) academic and intellectual also, it contains a kind of paradox, and both sides of this need to be recognised and accepted if the freedom of which mortals are capable (it is never total) is to develop richly and rewardingly.

Thinking of this college, I would define the paradox by saying that the liberation offered here is a liberation from the tyranny of permissiveness, both personal and intellectual. The fact that there is such a tyranny, and a very cruel one, is one of the clearest and yet the most reluctantly faced of all facts about present-day society.

It isn't really a paradox, and certainly not a contradiction: in principle, it's a fact of universal human experience. It's only under some kind of law—which necessarily means some initial abrogation of freedom—that freedom itself can ever flourish. One would like to disbelieve this: one would like to believe in a world in which each individual's immediate impulses could always we followed out at once, without frustration or conflict or other disaster. But all such thoughts only amount to nostalgia for the Garden of Eden, or perhaps to an anticipation of Heaven. It isn't at all ignoble that romantic minds should feel drawn towards anarchism. But in every situation that we know or can imagine in this life, it isn't a real option. Bad things rush in to fill every power-vacuum, and it often turns out that the only alternative to lousy government is even lousier government: any attempt at the too simply 'free' society—the anarchist society—will end up as a tyranny of the strong over the weak.

In public and political life, we all recognise this sad fact of our condition, accepting the necessity of law as a condition of any real freedom. The corresponding fact about personal and moral conduct is now starting to be discovered once again—after rather a bad patch—by many thoughtful and sensitive people. But the corresponding fact about academic and intellectual life is still too little recognised.

Many people would therefore be horribly shocked by this college. They might accept some part of its arrangements and life-style, perhaps grudgingly. There are rules here, there is discipline: it is not oppressive, but it is gently enforced. Civility and conduct are taken seriously, and the students are thereby paid a kind of compliment. Anybody who imagines fornication and drug-taking to be primary educational instruments, or who so despises the young as to consider their identity best expressed by dirt and rudeness, should look elsewhere for the enactment of his essentially contemptuous attitudes. It may well be conceded that there's a kind of liberation here: a liberation of parents, at least, from certain very familiar anxieties; a liberation of the young, also, from a social philosophy that elsewhere tends to belittle and degrade them.

But apart from these social and personal questions, there's another and deeper sense in which this college has really grasped the ambiguity or paradox of freedom, on lines that would give serious offence to some. These students work to a set programme or syllabus, their studies are laid down for them: only in the most marginal and minor way are they obliged to choose between different options or electives. More significantly still, the faculty have been chosen not from qualified graduates at large, but rather from such men and women as have already made a free intellectual commitment to a certain definable view of knowledge and of human destiny, and therefore of what liberal education is and what it's for.

Now a great many twentieth-century nerves are in such a condition that they will twitch—in horrified revulsion—at the first mention of such an educational and academic set-up. It sounds like a set rejection of that desperately important and fundamental thing, academic freedom: it suggests authoritarianism, dogma, forced indoctrination: words like 'Inquisition' and 'Fascism' will tremble at once on many lips.

In the whole of this field, there's a kind of hyper-sensitivity. I have known perfectly intelligent men to raise the cry of crypto-Naziism at any mention of that plainly necessary thing, 'law and order'. In vain do you point out to such a man that in every relevant sense, Hitler's Germany was one of the most 'disorderly' societies on record.

Such responses are, I think, slightly neurotic. They probably stem from the fact that the last few decades have seen an extraordinary flourishing of political and ideological tyranny, and of associated cruelties that were entirely vile. A decent man can only react against such things with revulsion. But because one was bitten by a dog in early childhood, it doesn't follow that he should thereafter build a life's philosophy upon the wickedness of all animals; and I want to suggest that one can over-react, or react imprecisely, against any evil force that seems to threaten the intellectual or academic kind of freedom. That there are such forces and that they are evil, I entirely agree. But freedom of this particular kind, if understood too crudely and without the counter-balancing presence of related but different values, can cease to be a friend of the intellectual life and the academic community and can become their most dangerous and sterilising enemy.

This is not a remote and theoretical possibility. It's something that has actually happened, not universally but very widely indeed: it is the factor chiefly responsible for the doubt and disarray in which most liberal education now finds itself.

On-campus life, in other words, is no exception to the general rule that freedom is a complex concept, and that the more simplistic and anarchical interpretations of it are self-defeating. A liberal education can educate the young *for* freedom, if it knows what human freedom is and what it's for: it will deprive them grievously if it tries too simply to educate them *by means of* freedom.

Such a deprivation can occur at any stage of the educational process. There is an old story of a small boy whose parents moved house, and who was therefore transferred from a grade-school at which things were actually *taught*—necessarily under a measure of loving discipline—to a school of the most thorough-going libertarian or clay-play-way variety. After a few days, he came to his mother in desperation. "Mummy, must I *always* do as I like in this horrible school?"

He wasn't being unreasonable. One of the prime requirements of the growing child is some kind of a structured and orderly environment: he needs to work out his place in the world, and he cannot do this if it's a world which gives at every pressure. And it's worth remembering that if that boy was obliged to continue at his clay-play-way school, he will quite certainly have grown up to join the vast army of those who are now proving to be functionally illiterate when the time comes for them to enter college.

That particular problem is a very serious one, but it might be considered soluble in principle. It might then be argued that while the young child needs some direction, this should be progressively reduced as he gets older. When college-time comes, should he not be mature enough to make his own choices and decisions?

So it is argued in fact, or—more usually—assumed: whatever may happen at the grade-school and high-school levels, it is taken for granted that a young man goes to college in order to learn what he chooses to learn. Hence, it is regarded as a thing very much in any college's favour if it offers him a wide choice of options, of diverse courses and credits. He is to receive a liberal education: as a *liberalis*, therefore, he must make his own free selection from what he finds on offer.

Now there are many senses in which nobody would wish to question this assumption. Its validity is, I would say, greatest at the more specialised university or post-graduate level: I am not so sure of its relevance to education of the more general or liberal kind, such as is concerned with the student's formation and development as a free human being, rather than with his training in some specialized art or science. (In order to avoid transatlantic misunderstandings and cross-purposes, it may be as well to observe that within the traditional British system, this kind of education was supposed to be the school's task and to be completed at about the age of eighteen. England has never possessed any exact equivalent of the American liberal arts college. The closest thing to it was perhaps the General or Pass Degree course offered by some universities. This was usually regarded as a 'poor relation' of the normal Honours course, a soft option for the weaker brethren; but now, as English schooling becomes less elitist and less intensive, something rather like it is coming back into favour.)

We all know that when it's a question of acquiring some definable and specialised skill, the student's freedom of choice is real but rather limited. If some medical student decides that anatomy and physiology are boring subjects, he can exercise a kind of freedom and decide not to study them. But in so deciding, he is simply choosing not to be a doctor after all. Options and specialisations do exist in that field; but basic medical science is what it is, a more or less fixed datum, and the student has to discipline himself and submit to its sometimes tedious requirements if he hopes to end up as a doctor.

But in many people's eyes, the great charm of liberal studies is precisely that they do *not* have that fixed, given, and ultimately 'servile' character, but leave the student wholly free. He must still accept the discipline of hard work: no kind of study can be accomplished fitfully, as one's idle moods may dictate. But a liberal education, precisely because it does not serve defined practical purposes outside itself, earns its title by being conducted in the greatest possible freedom—as regards the subjects studied, and also as regards the conclusions reached.

This view of the matter may seem like a truism. But when considered closely, it has implications which are (to put it mildly) controversial.

It is undoubtedly true that anybody will learn best and most easily when he's interested—that boredom is a major impediment to any kind of educational process. The ideal answer, perhaps, would be for every teacher to be in love with his subject, perpetually excited by it: there's something infectious about both excitement and boredom. The trouble is that such perfect teachers are none too common.

To this dilemma, it has long been conventional wisdom to say: "Well, since you are not constrained by the objective requirements of the specialized professions, choose the subjects which actually *do* interest you and study *them.*"

But this is putting the cart before the horse. To think like that is to confer the dignity of a final end upon the mere fact of studying, upon the educational process as such: the things studied then become the means, selected according to the degree to which they can facilitate that process. This might be regarded as a trivialisation of knowledge, of objective reality, psychologically undesirable in that it turns the student in on himself, putting him at the center of the picture. It also implies that he is the best judge of his own educational needs; and behind that, it carries the further and crucial implication that there is nothing which he actually *needs* to know—that there exists no natural order or hierarchy of intellectual disciplines, no objective and achieved 'wisdom' by which an older generation can hope to enrich and liberate a younger.

This is a philosophy of intellectual nihilism and defeat. It needs to be challenged; and initially, in connection with the student's freedom of choice. The faculty will have to wait their turn.

Napoleon described the English as a nation of shopkeepers, and with some justice: we are hardly in a position to be superior and derisive about the Americans if—as is sometimes alleged—they tend to see everything in commercial or mercantile terms.

Even so, I'm afraid I do find it rather amusing that American colleges should so often, and so naturally, choose the word 'catalogue' for the little book in which each one sets forth its courses and facilities. Where I live, such a book would be called the college's 'prospectus' or 'handbook' or 'calendar': the word 'catalogue' is a strictly commercial one, used by manufacturers and wholesalers and retailers with reference to the priced lists of the various commodities which they offer.

In the Supermarket

I must proceed cautiously: I have no desire to give offence. But I think we can see here a small symptom of something very American. One could think of other such symptoms. The English visitor to the United States is often surprised, for example, to find that the doctor or the pastor operates from an 'office': I have myself been slightly astounded to hear an American bishop refer to his cathedral and his seminary and all his other properties collectively as 'the diocesan plant'.

Well, I don't regard commercial and industrial activities as totally evil, and I don't think that the analogous use of their terminology offers any great insult to loftier activities. But the instinctive use of such terminology can be revealing; and I hope I may be allowed to suggest that American higher education has a clear tendency to see itself in commercial terms, with the college becoming a kind of instructional supermarket.

Such observations have often been made before. Some years ago, an English writer—married and adopted into American society—remarked that in her new country, "it is perilously possible to assume . . . that education is not an exercise, but a commodity, to be acquired in packages. The store is set up; one buys the goods; *et voilà*, an educated public."

Let nobody belittle the actual supermarket as an institution, or the ease with which one can there purchase any randomly-chosen selection of brightly-packaged commodities! Temperamentally in sympathy with the small shopkeeper, I usually find the greater convenience of the supermarket overwhelmingly attractive in practice—even though I do sometimes discover, later in the day, that I have shopped unwisely and on impulse. (Too often, it turns out that far more skill and dedication and love went into the package than into the product within: the technological and artistic brilliance of the one is poor compensation for the chemicalized tastelessness of the other. But I have already observed that our society is much more clever at means than at ends.)

In particular, I relish the freedom of choice offered by the supermarket. It can lead to bizarre results. I once saw a man pushing his cart to the check-out in order to pay for about thirty tins of dog-food and four bottles of champagne and nothing else whatever. My guess is that he possessed no dog, but had a philosophy of economising on food and *not* economising on drink. I can imagine worse philosophies.

By him and others like him, I am reminded of Evelyn Waugh's novel *The Loved One*, in which the dumb heroine is represented as having majored in Beauticraft, with Art and Philosophy and Chinese as her secondary subjects. Those were the bright packages which happened to catch her fancy as she wandered around bemusedly in the educational supermarket.

Waugh was, of course, indulging in sharp anti-American malevolence. But I think he put his finger here on a genuine weakness, and one of which the English are—or were—somewhat less guilty. In the British educational system, says the writer previously quoted, "the pattern in general is like that of a woven fabric, with all the threads of all the major subjects running continuously from beginning to end. In America, on the other hand, the pattern is more like that of the kind of open-work wall a child might build from a box of toy bricks; and the individual brick, the unit of education, is the 'credit' or 'course'."

This is perhaps a particular instance of something more general. An American writer has recently suggested that the dominant symbol of American life is that of standardized interchangeable parts in a totally fluid situation. One motel or one airport is exactly like every other: anybody can become President, anybody can become town dog-catcher: nothing and nobody really belongs anywhere.

To develop this theme would be both irrelevant and offensive, however; and I don't want to be too hard on the educational supermarket. In a highly mobile society, within which a student may have to put his education aside in Massachusetts and resume it in Utah, some degree of standardization—of interchangeability, of packaging—was perhaps inevitable; and if any young lady desires to load up her cart with Beauticraft, Art, Philosophy, and Chinese, I don't believe that her freedom to do so should be taken from her by Federal law.

But tricky problems arise when we try to relate this literal freedom of choice to the kind of 'freedom' which is implied in the idea of 'liberal' education.

Any tendency to see education in quasi-commercial terms

is, I think, likely to mislead us seriously. For one thing, the supermarket—or any other kind of shop or store—is very properly governed by the principle that 'the customer is always right'. The seller may advise: he cannot and should not compel. But any such analogy breaks down, on lines that may not be immediately apparent. When I go to the supermarket to buy supplies for the family, I *already know* something about food and cookery, a little about dietetics in relation to health, and a great deal about the tastes and requirements and fads of my household. The student who approaches the educational supermarket has no comparable advantages. In order to suggest his actual condition, one would need to imagine somebody going to the supermarket who has never entered such an institution before, will not (in practice) have a chance of entering one again, has not yet sampled any of the commodities on offer, and has only the haziest notion of the requirements which he hopes to satisfy.

Well, let there be full freedom of purchase under the law! But it will be agreed that a purchaser of the kind I've just suggested (and I admit that his literal situation strains credulity) will be wholly at the mercy of his own impulses and the bright packaging. It is most unlikely that the load which he finally takes home will be satisfactory by any possible standard.

In my capacity as a literary critic, I have to read a great many modern American novels; and one theme which recurs in them constantly is that of the disappointed and embittered college graduate. The lights were so bright, the shelves so full, the packages so alluring! But he came home with a miscellaneous collection of products which bore little relation to each other, or to the world, or to his own needs, or even to his own tastes, and even less to any scientific notion of a balanced and nourishing diet. So he abuses the institution, rather too savagely, for leading him so sadly astray. The real trouble is that he put too much faith in simple uninformed freedom; and now that he's discovered the insufficiency of this, it's too late for him to go back and try again.

Only fools (they say) learn by experience. The wise learn from the experience of others, and even from the collective experience of the species. But for some young people, this is rather galling: it means that they will have to learn from people older than themselves, and even from dead people.

Liberal education cannot usefully be conducted like a supermarket. It hopes to create, but it cannot presuppose, a situation in which wise choices can be made. A young man who was able to make wise choices would hardly *need* a liberal education: he would already possess the wisdom and judgment which such an education hopes to confer.

As we grope towards a notion of what liberal education ought to be, let us remember the supermarket as an image of what it should *not* be, and cannot be without radical failure. By definition, we are groping towards something which has something to do with some kind of freedom. But any great emphasis upon the first and most obvious kind of freedom—the student's freedom to study whatever takes his fancy—is going to prove self-destructive.

Newman lived before this happy age of supermarkets, but he used imagery of very much that kind to suggest the nature of the problem. Some writers, he explained, do not seem to understand what a university is. "They consider it as a sort of bazaar, or pantechnicon, in which wares of all kinds are heaped together in stalls independent of each other; and that to save the purchasers the trouble of running about from shop to shop; or an hotel or lodging-house where all professions and classes are at liberty to congregate, varying, however, according to the season, each of them strange to each, and about its own work or pleasure; whereas, if we would rightly deem of it, a University is the home, it is the mansion-house, of the goodly family of the sciences, sisters all, and sisterly in their mutual dispositions."

We know that sisters can squabble and fight upon occasion: their "mutual dispositions" are not always of the friendliest. But the relationship between them remains: it is something organic and objective, no arbitrary construction of social convention and the observing mind. Newman's words suggest that something similar may be true of the various subjects, disciplines, or fields of the academic task—that these may have mutual relationships of some objective kind, more "sisterly" than that provided by mere propinquity on the supermarket shelves, mere common availability to the random purchaser. "The simple question", he says elsewhere, "is whether the education sought and given should be based upon principle, formed upon rule, directed to the highest ends, or left to the random succession of masters and schools, one after another, with a melancholy waste of thought and an extreme hazard of truth."

These are noble words: they certainly suggest some kind of an answer to the problem, and for the student, some option less trivial and disappointing than the blind purchase of unrelated packages.

But they do so at a price. Principle? Rule? Ends? Truth? Such words will grate at once upon many academic nerves: they suggest some static and 'given' concept of reality and of education, some dogmatism which is to be imposed, an end to free enquiry, and anything which tends in that direction is to be rejected at once. Limits can perhaps be set upon the student's freedom of choice: he can be guided, he can even be gently pressured for his own good. But on the faculty side, intellectual and academic freedom is an absolute.

So it is said. But could this also be an over-simplification? Academic freedom is certainly a good thing. But does it need any kind of protection from itself?

Chapter IV:
SCEPTICISM AND THE ACADEMIC

Last night, by way of a change, I left this campus for the evening and attended a dinner-party. It was given by one of the faculty-members and his wife, with several children hovering around politely: two other faculty-members and their wives were my fellow-guests. It was a highly enjoyable occasion, "pastime with good company", helped along by the most loving kind of cookery and also by a delicate Californian wine.

But I wasn't only concerned to enjoy myself: I accepted that invitation in a spirit of keen curiosity. I have already mentioned the powerful impression which the students made upon me: now, I wanted to find out something about their teachers—about how these men conceived their task and tried to accomplish it. So I spent the evening listening and asking questions as well, and eventually formed a fairly clear picture—an intriguingly different picture from what you'll find on most other campuses.

I must emphasize, first of all, that these men do see themselves as *teachers*: it is their prime vocation to instruct the young, and they seem to have very little ambition in any other direction. This isn't quite the truism that it may seem to be. At most colleges and universities, my own included, the academic vocation includes various other things besides teaching. Outstandingly, it includes research: there is a fully institutionalised assumption that the best teacher of the young will be the man who is also active in the front line of his subject's advancement, so that the Ph.D. degree—which certifies a basic competence in research—becomes the academic's meal-ticket or qualification for office. Rather less formally, this assumption governs him thereafter, or at least until he has tenure: he has to continue as a researcher or at least as a writer, and 'publish or perish!' has become a gloomy joke.

This state of affairs may well be desirable at the specialist or postgraduate level; but so far as general or liberal education is concerned, I suspect that Newman may have been right in regarding teaching and research as radically different activities, calling for different talents and best undertaken by different people, perhaps in totally separate institutions. It is certainly possible for one man to have both vocations: my own tutor at Oxford, C.S. Lewis, was a profoundly original scholar and also a brilliant teacher, with an extraordinary talent for stimulating interest where boredom might otherwise have prevailed. But he was exceptional, and this is hardly surprising: it can only be by accident that two such very different skills co-exist in an individual.

These particular teachers are not required or encouraged to make themselves into researchers as well; nor are they encouraged to involve themselves in the larger world, as so many do elsewhere. This is a conspicuous development of our own time. Until quite recently, the popular image of the university teacher—the Oxford don, for example—was that of a retiring, possibly eccentric character, a proverbially absent-minded professor, immensely erudite in his own field, slightly innocent and unpractical elsewhere. But today's academic can entertain ambitions that correspond with a very different image. He can hope to appear as an 'expert' on television, to be interviewed by the press, to be asked for his sagacious opinion on public questions affecting his field (and, not infrequently, beyond it): he may well find himself profitaby involved in the affairs of big companies and corporations, or called in to advise the government and perhaps spend some time in its top-level service. Such possibilities differ, of course, according to the subjects and specializations of individuals; but in general, we can say that today's university is no isolated ivy-clad cloister, but rather an integral part of the great power-seeking world, offering considerable scope to that kind of ambition where it exists among the faculty. The instruction of the young is not necessarily neglected on this account: in practice, however, it does become just one among the university's preoccupations.

Here, it is the only preoccupation of the faculty: the anxious parent can feel assured that his son or daughter will be the prime object of their attention, and will not have to compete for this with the glitter of some plummy job in Washington or the absorbing interest of private research.

This means, of course, that the faculty are unlikely to be world-famous men. But where the faculty *are* world-famous men, it is inevitable that the individual student should find himself in very little contact with them. The tutorial system, as found at Oxford and Cambridge, is a partial exception; but on the average large American campus, the ordinary student gains little from his physical proximity to those great men. They are not preoccupied with him.

The different policy of this college means that I find here—very conspicuously—the family atmosphere to which so many institutions aspire and which so very few achieve. I apologize for this possibly sentimental cliché: I know something of families and of colleges too, and I can think of no better way of describing what I have found here. I hope I will not be understood to imply that family life is a kind of earthly paradise, devoid of all stress and difficulty.

But having described the faculty of this college as teachers above all else, I must now cope with this paradox, that, in a very real sense, they would indignantly repudiate any such title for themselves. Quite other people (they would say) do the real teaching of these students; and most if not all of them are dead.

Is there a touch of affectation here? I think not. A liberal education, as understood in the sense towards which I am groping, must profess to impart wisdom; and he would be a bold man —not to say an arrogant, conceited man—who declared himself to be wise *tout court*, qualified therefore to impart his own wisdom to the young.

Men of great wisdom do in fact exist; and it's possible in theory that your son or daughter might go to college and be instructed there by somebody destined for later recognition as the greatest thinker of all time—somebody wiser than Plato and Aristotle and Aquinas and Newton and Einstein all put together.

It is possible in theory, but one shouldn't bet on it: life being what it is, the vast majority of college instructors are going to be somewhat mediocre men. But we don't want our children taught by mediocrity, and we can't expect great wisdom from it.

The practical answer is clear enough. If liberal education is to impart wisdom, the real teachers will have to be the great minds of all time, with whom the student will make contact directly, through the great works of all times and all cultures, rather than through interpretations and commentaries. Possibly wise in his degree, the flesh-and-blood human teacher will then have a somewhat humble role to play: he will be an elder brother rather than a father, a senior fellow-student, and he will instinctively prefer to operate as the leader of a seminar or discussion-group of students rather than as a lecturer. He will hope to smooth the way and remove difficulties and provide particular information as needed, but without ever claiming to be the source of wisdom, the actual 'teacher'. Breadth and generosity of mind will be his prime qualifications, rather than specialized scholarship in some particular field: it will be better for him to have a good basic knowledge of all the subjects of the college curriculum, than to have very extensive knowledge of any one of them at the expense of the others.

Such a concept of liberal education, and of the college teacher's task, lies behind the various versions of the 'Great Books Programme' which have been developed in recent decades and in a number of institutions. The results have been impressive, provided that you don't ask too much: that is to say, such programmes provide an excellent basis for liberal education, so long as the end-product of this is defined (simply) as the well-read man or woman.

This is far from being an ignoble objective, but it leaves something out: unless supplemented, it will drive the poor student right back into the supermarket. It is all very well to say that the wisdom of our culture, and indeed of all cultures, is enshrined in the great books and also in the fairly wide consensus which exists as to which books *are* great. But these books say very different things. To take an obvious and perhaps extreme example, any well-compiled list of great books will have to include St. Augustine's *City of God* and also Karl Marx's *Das*

Kapital. Each is a great book by any standard, each has had incalculable influence upon thought and history: to be ignorant of either is to be an ill-educated man. But they represent totally different pictures of the human condition and of what is to be done about it: they contradict one another flatly at countless points, expressly or by clear implication: in so far as either is to be regarded as wisdom, the other has to be regarded—very considerably, if not completely—as folly.

If the student is conducted and helped through a Great Books Programme, this will go some substantial way towards making him a well-read man; and such an outcome is not to be belittled. But in what sense will he have learned the wisdom that liberates? He will have learned a great deal about what different ages and different individuals have regarded as wisdom: he will have become well-informed about the history of thought. But in his personal capacity, he will still be in the position of one who, in the supermarket, was confronted by countless bright and attractive packages and had no sound basis for choosing between them.

The conventional answer, of course is that having learned to think and having had so many intellectual options laid before him, he will be mature enough to make his own responsible choice between them.

Now I don't want to sound too cynical. But I think it's clear that while this could happen in theory, it very seldom happens in practice. Two other outcomes are far more usual. The accidents of circumstance and psychology may cause the student to make what must (in the last analysis) be regarded as a random choice: alternatively, the wide variety of human opinions may drive him into a fundamental scepticism, which will in practice leave him defenceless against the violent pressures of intellectual and cultural fashion. In either case, liberal education will have failed in its task of imparting the wisdom appropriate to a free and rational man; and sad experience tells us that it very commonly does so fail, the graduate being as well-read and well-informed as one could wish, but remaining enslaved to his own whims or else to the mere trend of the moment.

He needed, I suspect, some 'teacher' of a third kind: those human teachers to begin with, and those greater teachers whom he meets in the great books; and then, guiding the former and providing the basis for evaluating the latter, something else.

But what shall it be? Is there in fact any objective and achieved wisdom, distinct from the wide variety of human opinion and providing a standard by which this can be judged?

It seems to me that a negative answer to that question will rule out the possibility of a genuinely liberal education. But it seems equally clear that any positive answer to that question is going to set limits to 'academic freedom' on the faculty side, as that phrase is commonly understood today. Will this be a totally bad thing?

The experience of last night's dinner party enables me to allay one kind of fear at the outset. I was among men who understand their own academic freedom in a distinctly unusual sense, subjecting this to what they very definitely do regard as an objective and achieved wisdom, a 'dogmatism' if you like. Some would therefore expect them to be narrow-minded bigots. I wish to report that they are not in the least like that. They speak like free men.

What kind of an absolute is academic freedom? And what does it mean?

We can all agree that within the college or university, as elsewhere in the field of human relationships, there are many possibilities of tyranny and oppression and injustice, against which the rights of the individual need to be cherished and defended. But when people talk about 'academic freedom', they usually mean something different. It's not merely injustice to the individual that they fear: it's an obstruction or deflection of the intellectual process, and a consequent frustration—on whatever scale—of the whole purpose for which the academic community exists. It exists for learning, for the discovery and dissemination of truth; and this is a task that can only be undertaken fruitfully in an atmosphere of complete intellectual freedom.

It is a formidable argument. Its strength lies in the fact that reality is complex and cannot be fully grasped by any individual. All possible roads to it must therefore be kept open, even those which are currently assumed to be impossible roads. Each inquirer will have his own contribution to make, his own particular angle on the relevant area of reality; but he will also have his own prejudices and limitations, and these will need to be complemented and corrected by the findings of others. Some lines of thought, after beginning confidently, will prove sterile: others will have to be tested at every point, and will still remain open to radical question that will itself be under question. And so, by a never-ending dialectical process, by the free courteous conflict of different approaches and different hypotheses, a synthesis will emerge progressively, one which will have an increasingly close correspondence with reality.

So it is argued, with real but—I suggest—clearly limited cogency. Any such statement of the case for academic freedom, as commonly understood, presupposes a 'model' of intellectual activity which corresponds fairly well with the actual pattern of some disciplines but hardly at all with the pattern of others. Its greatest correspondence is with those disciplines which are most clearly progressive or cumulative in their methods—with the empirical sciences above all. These really do develop, and by a dialectical process which really does need to be untrammeled: scientists are as capable as other men of prejudice and limited vision, but any errors so arising can always be corrected by further experiment in other quarters, unless this process is impeded by authoritarianism, by dogma, by the power of the scientific 'Establishment'. (Arthur Koestler and others have shown that it can in fact be so impeded, and quite often is.)

So the empirical sciences develop, extending the area of our reasonably certain knowledge enormously, reducing the area of our ignorance measurably. But can we say anything remotely similar about (say) philosophy?

I don't see how we can. As it exists in the academic world, it seems quite unrealistic to think of philosophy as a growing body of more or less certain knowledge, needing to be developed overall and to be corrected here and there in detail. The actual academic scene shows us a very different picture. We see any number of brilliant minds at work, but in radical conflict with one another: we see new approaches and methods being invented constantly and becoming extremely fashionable, but never reigning for long without radical challenge. Every year there are more books to study, and in that sense philosophy is a developing subject, with those changing fashions providing ample material for the thesis-writer and the controversialist and for all those who enjoy intellectual excitement for its own sake. The idealism of Bradley was in, and then it was out; logical positivism rose and shone and fell; metaphysics was killed and people danced on its grave, but then it treacherously crept forth and started to show signs of life once again. It was all great fun; but what did it all add up to? Certainly not to any growing *corpus* of solid agreed certainty, comparable to the 'knowledge explosion' of the scientists.

In this rather embarrassing situation, the academic discipline of philosophy has tended to become the discipline of studying philosophers. It is no rare thing to meet a man who has majored or graduated in this field, and who is splendidly erudite about what everybody has said, from the Sophists through Descartes up to Wittgenstein and beyond, but who remains a total sceptic as regards all the matters about which those numerous men were striving for certainty.

Some present-day philosophers would welcome this inconclusive conclusion: they would say that while we cannot know the 'truth' (if indeed it 'exists') we can at least know and study what various men have thought about the truth. But it then becomes pertinent to ask why we should bother to do so. Most or all of the people concerned, the famous philosophers, actually did suppose themselves to be finding the truth, or at least moving some way towards its discovery. If, from the standpoint of our own scepticism, we declare all this to have been an illusion, we shall be saying in effect that they were not wise men at all, but self-deluding fools of the most egregious sort. The study of their thoughts and writings can then only be undertaken sardonically: it will become nothing more than study in human folly. As such, it may still be able to sharpen the mind for servile purposes: as a university discipline, it may help us to get good computer-programmers and also a few ironic novelists of sharp nihilistic quality. I have come across some of these—so trained, so disillusioned.

This nettle is seldom grasped, but it needs grasping. We are talking about the possibility of some objective and achieved wisdom, as against all guess and hunch and opinion, and about philosophy—which means 'the love of wisdom'—as a means of finding it. In this connection, we are trying to evaluate what most men call 'academic freedom'. Well, has this paid off? Has it achieved concrete results? After decades and centuries of academic endeavor, has it yielded even a small core of ascertained and agreed truth? If so, the young are entitled to be told what it is; and in this case, academic freedom will have to contract in scope, since it can hardly include a freedom to tell lies or to conceal truth. But if not, what kind of value can we attach to the philosophical enquiry? How would we assess (say) a chemist, if he told us that while one can always play amusing games in the laboratory, there isn't any real chemical knowledge at all? How *can* the philosophy-dons offer social justification for their tenure, their salaries, their freedom?

I have therefore reached a possibly challenging conclusion, which ties in well with my own experience. Academic freedom, as currently understood, is a real value and of great importance to certain disciplines—to the sciences, broadly speaking, and to other disciplines in so far as these have quasi-scientific elements and implications and therefore develop on cumulative or progressive lines. But where philosophy is concerned—and any other discipline in so far as it has philosophical elements and implications—this is a self-contradictory and self-destructive concept unless heavily qualified. Philosophy has to be a manner of coming to know reality. If it fails to have this character, it becomes a mere trivial word-game. But in so far as it succeeds, in so far as reality becomes known, it limits our freedom to think and teach what we like.

This last point is important. I have already quoted the words of Jesus, "The truth shall make you free", and I accept them as—among other things—a basic statement of what 'liberal education' has to mean. But there is a crude and ignoble sense in which the converse is more obviously true. The ignorant man is (in a way) free to think what he likes: increasing knowledge will reduce that kind of freedom. At this moment, I am myself 'free' to believe anything I like about (say) brain-surgery, or the economics of Nicaragua. I am also, and for that reason, totally unable to *do* anything about either of those important matters. If I chose to get educated about either of them, the process would involve a progressive diminution of my present glorious freedom of belief. But it would also involve a progressive liberation from my present ignorance, my present inability to act. I would thus become a free man, in fields where I am now crippled and helpless; but for this freedom, I would have to pay the price of accepting the determinate and objective nature of reality in those fields, and conforming my mind to it. I would become more free in one way, less free in another.

And so we get back to the great paradox of freedom. We know that our political freedom can only exist under law: something similar turns out to be true of our intellectual and academic freedom. If all things are to be perennially in doubt, then the mind is going to be crippled, hog-tied, enslaved to its own ignorance. Any beginnings of free thought and free action must depend upon the prior establishment of at least a limited area of certainty, which we will naturally hope to be—or to become—as extensive as possible. But the paradox remains. If such an area exists, in so far as it gets extended, the undesirable kind of freedom will have to be sacrificed: we shall not be able, without dishonesty, to think as we please.

Let me approach this teasing paradox from a different angle. If we treat academic freedom as an absolute, we shall be presupposing a fundamental scepticism: we shall be taking it for granted that while we have this man's opinion and that man's hunch, nothing is really *known*, nor ever can be. The trouble is that anybody who thinks like this, and desires the academic life to be conducted accordingly, is himself taking up a particular philosophical position and trying to impose it upon others. Fundamental scepticism is itself a dogma, and a very questionable one: its present dominance on many of our campuses may blind us to the two obvious objections that can be raised against it.

The first is that it is self-contradictory. This goes for all scepticisms, and notably for logical positivism of the old Vienna School type: this could never be formulated except in sentences which declared themselves to be meaningless. I remember once reading a philosopher-cum-physiologist who asserted that the mind cannot know anything outside itself. He had reached this conclusion by studying the brain and the physiology of perception. But what reason had he got for supposing that the brain and the optic nerve actually exist?

Then, it must be remembered that fundamental scepticism down-grades the academic person while claiming to secure his freedom. If all things are to be perennially in doubt, always open to radical question, then he ceases to be philosopher, a seeker and (in some measure) a finder of the truth. He continues to be a man whom we can use for servile purposes; he also provides us with word-games and other petty amusements. Let him be paid to continue doing so. But he isn't such a great man as we once thought he was.

Fundamental scepticism can, perhaps, be chosen by an intelligent man as his own philosophical position. (I'm not entirely sure that it can be actually *believed*: but let that pass for the moment.) But if it is so chosen, the consequence that follows is not "Since we are in so much doubt, let all academic enquiries be conducted in an atmosphere of total freedom." The more logical consequence is "Let us abandon all academic enquiry and close down all the universities, apart from those fields and departments which are strictly pragmatic and allow for empirical verification at every point. We can allow the doctors and engineers to remain at work: servile studies may continue, provided that they show results and are cost-effective. But studies of the supposedly liberal kind—those which claim to be worth pursuing for their own sake, being concerned with the nature and destiny of man and the apprehension of reality, with wisdom—must now be regarded as a mere beating of the air, an indulgence in private fantasy and self-deception. They may provide some people with aesthetic experiences and cultural activities, and can be cautiously tolerated at that rather trivial level. But in so far as they make any loftier claim—in philosophy above all—they are pure nonsense and will have to go."

If we reject this practical conclusion, we shall have to qualify our scepticism and agree that reality can actually be known in some measure; and unless we want academics to be liars or concealers of known reality, we shall then have to accept some limitation upon their absolute freedom.

Will they then become the unhappy victims of intellectual tyranny? Will they become narrow-minded bigots? Possibly, here and there. But I have more than the experience of a single dinner-party to assure me that such dangers are not overwhelming and inescapable.

Chapter V:
PIGS IS PIGS

What kind of image will most aptly suggest the distinctive happiness which I observe in these rather unusual students? An image (I think) of liberation; and I have titled this book accordingly. Most colleges and universities today provide excellent education of the servile kind; but along with this, most of them provide also an indoctrination in scepticism, and this is something which paralyzes and imprisons the mind. But these particular young people have been set free.

Other images could of course be used to suggest their condition: images of food after long starvation, for example. But what haunts my mind at this moment is an image of dry land and firm ground underfoot, after a long struggle in stormy waters. The ship sank, let us say, and not all the passengers were good swimmers: they splashed and flapped around in disorientation and despair, flung in this direction and that by random wave-patterns, and some went under. But for the lucky ones, there came a moment of near-miracle. The storm continued, but they were out of it: God or good fortune had unexpectedly thrown them up onto a friendly shore. Nourishment and rescue would now be available; but for the moment they concentrated on that sheer delight of having solid earth to walk on and being able to get their bearings.

Their delight was not unmixed, even now: they were still very much concerned about those who were still lost and desperate in the cruel sea. With a strong sense of urgency, therefore, they tried to work out some way of using their own more fortunate position for purposes of rescue. They might or might not succeed. But they at least were safe; and they knew that while rescuers sometimes have to take risks, you don't help a drowning man if you jump back into the water and drown alongside him. He needs something more concrete and particular and practical than mere human solidarity and a sharing in the existential anguish of death. He needs to be pulled out: he needs to find firm ground underfoot.

Now there are many circles in which any such image of the educational process—or of intellectual activity in general—would arouse strong hostility and objection: as I have already suggested more than once, fundamental scepticism has (in our time) become something like an established orthodoxy. This rejection of my Robinson-Crusoe image would be partly philosophical. It would be agreed that people who are actually drowning have got to be rescued if possible. But it would be denied firmly and even furiously that there is any corresponding duty—or even any corresponding possibility—in connection with the life of the mind and the knowledge of reality. Here (it would be said) there *is* no dry land, no objectively firm ground underfoot, capable of being recognized as such: those who believe that there is are deluding themselves.

I shall return to this curious notion later. In the meantime, I would like to point out that the rejection of my image would not be *simply* philosophical. Having frequently been engaged in this particular battle, I can assure you that it would also include psychological and *ad hominem* elements, even moral elements. The implied 'dogmatism' would not only be rejected as being erroneous: it would also be rejected as a social evil, a kind of tyranny, indicating bad and possible pathological motivations in those who advocate it. Yes, there is much storm and stress in human life. But if you try to drag others onto that imaginary dry land of yours, this can only be because of your secret desire to dominate, your disregard for opinions other than your own! It is—in fact—only timid and emotionally insecure people, sad cases of arrested development, who even desire that supposed security of firm ground underfoot. Anyone of full maturity should be able to accept the storm with courage, the relativity and ultimate uncertainty of all things.

So it would be said: so I have often heard it said, and I cannot be the judge of how justly it is said about myself.

It needs to be pointed out, however, that the motivations-game can be played in both directions. If we are going to get psychological at all, we can reasonably get psychological about the motivations of those who so passionately *want* the dogma of fundamental scepticism to be true, as well as the motivations of their opponents.

I do not not want to make any sweeping accusation, certainly not of individuals. But it is too easily forgotten that writers and academics and the intelligentsia in general have a direct personal 'interest' in scepticism. This will not govern the thinking of honest men, but it will constitute what religious people call a 'temptation' for many: some will resist the temptation manfully, some weakly, and some (perhaps) not at all. We live in a permissive society, after all: the idea of resisting temptation is out of fashion.

The nature of this particular temptation needs to be considered. Ideally at least, the intellectual—in the university and elsewhere—is a professional seeker of the truth: he is also a man skilled in the use of the mind. He is paid to deploy that skill, and he enjoys doing so.

But a fondness for intellectual enquiry is not at all the same thing as a hunger for the truth. The two may appear similar; but so far as the enquirer's motivations are concerned, they are in direct conflict. In so far as truth is actually attained in any matter, the enquiry is—to that extent—over. So, to that extent, is the particular and most rewarding kind of excitement which the enquiry provided.

Consider fox-hunting. Watching the riders and the hounds as they go streaming across the English shires on a winter afternoon, you might suppose that they actually *wanted* the fox. Perhaps the hounds do, but the riders certainly don't: what they want is the thrill of the chase, and when the fox is finally caught and demolished, the fun is over for the time being.

That's all very well on the hunting-field, but it creates a fatal kind of schizophrenia on campus. How often we have all met the learned man who is professionally committed to hunting for the truth, but intensely hostile to any suggestion that it might actually be captured, once and for all! It's very understandable: in so far as truth actually gets attained, the seeker of it finds himself out of a job. The fox is dead, the enjoyable hunt is over.

It would be a mistake to press this cynical point too far. But all men have their particular temptations, and these are often occupational; and it needs to be recognized that the intellectual—as such—is chronically tempted to what might be called the sin of philosophical contraception. He wants to enjoy the legitimate pleasures of intellectual enquiry, but he is reluctant to be burdened with that activity's natural end-product, which is the knowledge of reality. He therefore takes steps—perhaps quite subconsciously—to sterilize his enquiry in advance by the adoption of relativist or sceptical philosophies. The lovers' play can thus continue forever, unimpeded by pregnancy and childbirth: the huntsman can thus enjoy the chase forever, knowing that the fox won't ever get caught. But the love-making and the hunt will both be fakes.

How far the intelligentsia yield to this temptation, we don't know and probably shouldn't ask: that they yield to it sometimes and in some degree is a matter of observation. What needs to be borne steadily in mind (in all charity) is the fact that they are *subject to* the temptation—that where fundamental scepticism is in question, as against some possibility of coming to know reality finally and definitely, they are interested parties, biassed by the fact of their occupation. (There is a political version of the same temptation. It has often been observed that the intelligentsia have a strong tendency to take the 'progressive' or leftist side in any disputed matter—so much so that a 'conservative intellectual' seems almost a contradiction in terms. Some would see this tendency in terms of superior minds perceiving the greater merits of the 'progressive' case. But here again, the intelligentsia are interested parties. In so far as some kind of revolutionary change is called for, there will need to be a great deal of re-thinking, which will give them a prominent role and function. But in so far as what we need is greater fidelity to some long-established tradition, they won't have so much to do and they won't be so important. Excessive cynicism here would be uncharitable. But a total absence of cynicism would be unrealistic.

Intellectuals as such are no worse than the rest of us. But their personal situation does predispose them to favour certain definable kinds of answer to a wide range of questions; and the possession of a a first-class brain is no guarantee of total integrity, total objectivity, total neutrality before the facts.)

Is there really any firm ground on which the mind of man can stand with well-justified confidence? Let us agree that there are many kinds of false or illusory certainty; that some people who suppose themselves to be standing on firm ground are actually drowning; that dogmatic assertiveness can spring from a desire to dominate; that cravings for security and assurance can sometimes be pathological. But the case for scepticism is not thereby established. Comparable *ad hominem* charges can be made in the opposite sense too: the motivations-game can be played in both directions, and the accusations so made will cancel one another out, leaving us with the objective question, which still needs to be considered on its merits.

What might those be? We can certainly guess and theorize forever. But can we really *know* reality or any part of it, such as the nature and destiny of man? If not, the idea of liberal education seems to me to become a mere delusion. What does it become in fact, among people who don't seem to believe in anything at all—not even the workings of their own minds, not even the evidence of their own senses?

Last summer, two young American friends came to my home, which is near London, and we discussed all manner of things. Both were pleasant and bright, and both were philosophy majors from liberal arts colleges of repute. The conversation developed on such lines that I eventually plucked up my courage and uttered the Chestertonian dogma 'Pigs is pigs'; and to this, both my young friends responded with a storm of contradiction and even of anger. No, I was quite wrong: the mind cannot know anything outside itself, and it certainly mustn't classify its experiences in any essentialist language of objective pighood.

And so on. But soon it was time for them to go, and they started worrying about the time of their train. I pointed out, mildly, that since there was no real and knowable world within which their train could have any objective 'out there' existence, their anxiety was misplaced. This irritated them a little: philosophy (I was given to understand) was one thing, but the practical business of daily life was another.

"So you don't actually *believe* that sceptical philosophy of yours, in the sense of governing your lives by it?"

No, of course they didn't: when pressed, they admitted that for them and their instructors too, philosophy amounted to little more than a word-game, making no real claim to yield 'truth'.

I scented hope. I knew already that they were unhappy people, bright enough at the superficial and social level but bitter and alienated within, according to a widely prevalent pattern of bitterness and alienation; and I had long suspected that many troubles of that kind, apparently psychological in nature, are philosophical by origin. Split your mind into two halves, a discursive half and a practical half, and give them radically incompatible things to believe: the outcome is going to be interior conflict or stress. Too many people, finding themselves so troubled, run straight off to the nearest analyst: a good teacher of language and logic might provide them with a more health-giving therapy.

In that spirit of clinical benevolence, I therefore begged this young couple to start being sceptical about their own scepticism. Could we discuss this? Could we at least define our terms?

But I was too late: already they were off to that momentary appearance in the experienced flux of becoming which (for some reason) they insisted on treating just as though it could be known and used as a real train. And as they left me, I saw the same expression on both faces: it was an unmistakeable expression of fear. I had rattled them.

"The truth shall make you free"? I have heard that long-term prisoners are sometimes terrified of release, and therefore commit some further crime before long so as to get safely back inside.

I cannot prove that fundamental scepticism is untrue. Nobody can prove anything except on some basis of agreed premises; and any premises that are capable of being put into words are also capable of being verbally questioned. Any argument whatsoever can thus be made into an infinite regress—a happy outcome indeed, if your chief desire is that it should go on for ever.

In many kinds of discussion, however, there comes a point at which the question of sanity takes precedence over the question of demonstrable truth. I have just suggested that psychological problems may have philosophical roots: the converse can also be true. Imagine some man who swears that there's a world-wide conspiracy against him, and interprets all public events in terms of this. You can't possibly prove him wrong; and you have to admit that in the strictest logical sense, it is possible—that is, it involves no contradiction—that there should indeed be such a conspiracy. You point out, feebly, that you can see no evidence of any such thing: but he is ready with his reply. "Do you think these people work openly? Would you expect their agents to reveal themselves? They're a long sight cleverer than that, I can assure you!"

You'll never win the argument, you'll never prove him wrong. But you know perfectly well that you're in the presence of a paranoid.

There are certain pathological states—some of them permanent, some of them induced temporarily by drugs or fever or exhaustion—in which the mind loses its grip on reality and slips into the void, so that all physical objects and even the perceiving self dissolve into a terrifying nightmare of unreality and menace. Were I in such a state, down by the lakeside under this Californian sun, I might indeed perceive the ducks as monsters or apes or devils, or as everything, or as nothing at all; and if I so described them, you wouldn't be able to prove me wrong. But you would recognize that I was in a pathological state of some kind.

In our time, there's a widespread and possibly morbid interest in such matters. In my work as a literary critic, I am constantly coming across novels and other books—certain types of science-fiction, in particular—which indicate that the writer has, and expects his reader to have, a powerfully schizoid imagination. Many people nowadays seem to find madness more interesting than sanity, and I take this to be a bad sign of the times. It has an interesting precedent. Chaucer lived in the high civilization of the Middle Ages, and as far as I can remember, there isn't a single madman in the whole body of his voluminous works—though there are any number of villains. But when we get to that period of stress and breakdown which is optimistically called the Renaissance, all literature suddenly begins to be full of lunatics.

No, I cannot *prove* that ducks are ducks, or that pigs are pigs, or that there are both resemblances and differences between ducks and pigs, capable of being put into truthful words. No such proof is either necessary or possible. Such questions are not philosophical at all: they concern the presence or absence of the broad basic sanity which makes philosophy (or any other coherent activity) possible. I have suggested that certain psychological problems could be eased by intervention and help of the philosophical kind: I want to suggest now that fundamental scepticism, *where it is fully believed*, is a pathological condition and calls for intervention and help of the psychiatric kind.

That emphasized qualification is important: without it, I might lay myself open to a great many libel-actions, for suggesting that a great many distinguished academics are insane. I don't suppose that they are; or at least, not more frequently than other people. My charge against them is a different one, though it might still be actionable if I were rash enough to give names. The trouble isn't that they're insane: it's that they're pretending. For lecture-room purposes, they affect a kind of uncertainty which they forget completely when they're in the outside world of trains and ducks. If they retained it there, if they conducted normal life on a basis of *real* epistemological doubt, they would be recognized at once as psychiatric cases.

Both 'being' and 'knowing' are mysteries, capable of infinite analysis. But both are also manifest realities of the simplest kind.

Why then do so many brilliant men, not schizophrenic or otherwise off their heads, talk otherwise? I can think of three reasons.

In the first place—and here I am very much in sympathy with them—the epistemological pseudo-problem is a word-game of the most fascinating and paradoxical kind. I adore all such games, and indulge in them shamelessly: for example, I can prove to you by algebra that 1 equals 2. I can also prove that nothing whatsoever exists, with particular cogency when I'm helped along by a couple of martinis. Give me two more, and I'll probably be able to work out a conclusive proof that a duck is really a pig. Thus we can enjoy ourselves, in a nice irresponsible way. The danger comes when we play such games in the presence of young people who are likely to take them seriously; and it won't always be averted by our frank statement that they *are* games. My two young friends had been so warned, quite explicity, but this didn't prevent their philosophical education from leaving them mentally hog-tied.

Secondly, and more seriously, I must repeat the psychological and *ad hominem* accusation at which I hinted earlier. The concept of actually known reality is a burdensome one, even an alarming one, and not only for those people who make their living by chasing a fox that must never be finally caught. Doubt, when carefully rationalised and nourished and sustained, is a splendid defence-mechanism against it.

And then there is that vague but pervasive feeling that it's somehow modest and democratic to express doubt, but assertive and dictatorial to express certainty. This goes very far. At any moment now, we'll have some mathematician saying that while he doesn't want to be dogmatic, he does feel that from some points of view, it might be meaningful to suggest that 1 plus 1 equals 2.

Education is (among other things) a process of growing up: it takes away the child's freedom of ignorance and gives us the adult's better freedom of knowledge. But it can only do this in so far as knowledge is in fact available; and it can only be 'liberal' in so far as we do have real knowledge about the nature and destiny of man. Ducks are a good starting-point, but they aren't enough.

From this, there follows a principle which is resoundingly at variance with the dominant thought of our time: to many, it would seem like a mere paradox or even a flat contradiction. It is the principle that *liberal education must necessarily be dogmatic*. It needs to be based upon the axiom that "the truth shall make you free", and must therefore presuppose some antecedent grasping of fundamental truth. If it tries to base itself upon the converse notion, seeing freedom as a necessary precondition for the seeking of a truth which still remains to be found, it will work peripherally but fail centrally. The empirical sciences will do well enough. But in deeper matters, including the philosophy and use of those sciences, there will be no criterion by which thought can be assessed: erudite in particular matters, the students will then be fundamentally at sea. Those struggling survivors of shipwreck, in the image cited earlier, were not free men: they were wholly at the mercy of the winds and the waves and their own terror. It was only those who were swept ashore onto firm ground who could then take stock, and evaluate their position, and make free decisions, and in general enjoy some degree of liberty.

To deny the existence of firm ground is to deny all such possibilities: fundamental scepticism is the enemy of liberal education. Where it prevails, we may still be able to train highly efficient slaves. But we shall have nothing but petty amusement to offer to free men, or to men who hope to be free, or to slaves in their brief hours of leisure. We shall be able to say plenty about means but nothing about ends. We shall know how to build bridges, but not how to make your decision about whether to cross some bridge or not: we shall know how to keep patients alive, but not how to decide whether life is worth living.

My two young philosophy majors illustrate the point beautifully. They had each received a 'liberal education' as the phrase is currently understood, at the hands of well-qualified men in institutions of high repute. And the end-product in each of them was a fundamental confusion of the mind—a 'philosophy' which resolved itself into mere word-games and could not possibly be taken seriously in daily life.

They were still nice people, though not particularly happy people. But mentally, they seemed to me to be wholly enslaved, wholly at the mercy of such sub-rational influences as the fashion and trend of the time, the influence of the powerful media, and their own glandular and psychological pressures. If some new Hitler were to come along, skilled at the art of manipulation and propaganda, they would be mentally defenceless against him. In many senses—that political sense included—their enormously expensive 'liberal education' had failed totally.

Pigs is Pigs

An illiterate peasant might well be a better philosopher, in the sense of being a more effective lover of wisdom. He would know at least that pigs are pigs.

Learning from him, let us now grasp the first of the two great dogmatisms proposed in this book, not as the findings of free enquiry, but as the necessary firm ground which makes free enquiry possible.

This is the dogma that pigs is indeed pigs; that fundamental scepticism is untrue; that reality is real, exists independently of our perceptions of it, can be known (within limits, but certainly) by ourselves, and can be made the subject of statements or predictions which (again within limits) can be true or false and can be known to be so.

Call this an arbitrary dogma if you will: it might be called common-sense or sanity. It is quite certainly the necessary starting-point for any real and effective freedom of the mind: it by-passes the infinite-regress word-game of epistemological doubt, giving us an initial foothold upon firm ground. Without this, we cannot think at all.

The point was well made by G.K. Chesterton, writing many years ago about St Thomas Aquinas. "Even those who appreciate the metaphysical depth of Thomism in other matters have expressed surprise that he does not deal at all with what many now think the main metaphysical question: whether we can prove that the primary act of recognition of any reality is real. The answer is that St Thomas recognized instantly, what so many modern sceptics have begun to suspect rather laboriously, that a man must either answer that question in the affirmative, or else never answer any question; never ask any question; never even exist intellectually, to answer or to ask. I suppose it is true in a sense that man can be a fundamental sceptic; but he cannot be anything else: certainly not even a defender of fundamental scepticism."

This might be called a brisk substitution of common-sense for the uncommon nonsense that passes too widely for philosophy: it certainly contains an implied threat to the livelihood of many an academic word-spinner, and might be resented accordingly. But it does set the mind free, enabling it to start work constructively and in the realistic hope of getting somewhere. The possibility of a liberal education begins here: this is the point at which we first struggle ashore from our old helplessness in the chaotic seas of doubt and denial.

It is of course a dogma, in the sense that it has to be experienced and asserted: it cannot possibly be proved. But if liberal education is to be restored, the first thing to go must be the old fallacy that 'dogma' and 'freedom' are antithetical terms. They are not. As Chesterton says elsewhere, speaking of that same Dominican dogmatist: "It will not be possible to conceal much longer from anybody the fact that St Thomas Aquinas was one of the great liberators of the human intellect."

Chapter VI:
WHO CLAIMS TO KNOW?

So I sit here once again, down by the lake, and contemplate the ducks that were my starting-point. In their reality, as in the related but different reality of pigs, I see humanity's prime escape from the prison of scepticism, our first hope of an education that will not be essentially servile.

I know various facts about a duck: if I studied for many years and became a world-famous duckologist, I would come to know a great many more. But in the meantime, here and now, each duck itself—as distinct from facts about it—is the direct object of my limited but genuine knowledge; and it is at this point that I first find dry land under my feet. The prime object of the intellect is reality, not ideas about reality.

In that basic and desperately important sense, the foundations of a liberal education might perhaps be best laid by a sustained period of hard—and even slave-like—work on the farm.

But this can hardly be the whole story. Let it be conceded that the mind can apprehend reality, in principle at least: has it ever done so in fact, in any deeper and more far-reaching sense? The free man is concerned with ends rather than means, and therefore with the nature and purpose of human existence; and about such matters, a wide variety of opinions have in fact been held. We can certainly cause the young to become well-informed about those opinions. But has the long process of experience and enquiry and debate borne any more substantial fruit? Have we actually found anything out? Do we (in any possible sense) *know the answers*? Is there in fact any body of achieved wisdom, of truth, which can be handed on to the young as their liberation from the tyranny of mere opinion and scepticism?

If we answer such questions negatively, liberal education will become nothing more than a training in the cultural elegances; and in a society as fragmented as our own, it will then inevitably retain its present incoherence, its tendency to generate disappointment and bitterness in those subjected to it.

Now a great many people are conspicuously prejudiced against any positive findings in this respect, and not only for the ignoble reasons suggested in the last chapter. About the ultimate nature and purpose (if any) of human existence, those various opinions are in fact held; and to many, it seems somehow undemocratic to pick on one of them and exalt this to the standing of an achieved wisdom, a known set of answers, at the expense of all the others. Surely we're all entitled to our own viewpoints? Surely one man's opinion is as good as the next man's? Why should any minority regard its views as particularly sacred?

On such lines as these, any scepticism or relativism about the ultimates can be made to seem admirable. It is humble, as against the pride of all dogmatists; it is broad-minded, as against the bigots; it is tolerant, as against the Inquisitors.

Unfortunately, it is also self-destructive: it hangs itself with its own rope. Any such scepticism is also the complacent dogmatism of a minority, and is therefore in no position to rebuke the similarly complacent dogmatisms of other minorities. The sad fact is that *whatever* view you take of reality and the human condition, you have to cope with the fact that a very large number of people don't share it. Each of the great religions and each of the great political ideologies is a minority-view, when statistically considered; and this goes for scepticism as well. It may seem very deplorable to say "We are right, and everybody else is wrong: we are therefore going to make sure that the university scene is dominated by our beliefs, with dissenting voices kept marginal if not silenced altogether." But the offence—if offence it be—is committed by the doctrinaire sceptic, no less than by the doctrinaire Catholic or the doctrinaire Marxist. Most people don't agree with him, any more than with those others.

Who Claims to Know?

Arrogance is a fault of which any man can be guilty. But if we are to say anything at all about the human condition and the destiny of a free man, we shall need to overcome that neurotic feeling that nobody must ever be found and declared mistaken. The wide variety of conflicting views makes it clear that a great many people *are* mistaken in one way or another, in one degree or another; and there is nothing necessarily arrogant in the attempt to discover which ones they are. Heresy-hunting is not called for: the object of the enquiry should be truth itself and for its own sake, rather than the failure of others to perceive it. But we must be prepared to accept the fact of that failure—to climb down humbly when we ourselves are found mistaken, and also (a harder thing, perhaps, in the present climate of opinion) to stand by in apparent complacency when the other party has to climb down.

People matter, and there must always be great gentleness and respect for their feelings. But neither the college nor the intellectual arena in general is primarily a school of courtesy. A higher and objective purpose comes first: liberal education must be conducted courteously, but it will only be itself when conducted as though the thing that mattered was truth.

What kind of truth matters most? What kind of truth can be offered as centrally important fact and not as mere opinion?

In the previous chapter, I mentioned two great dogmatisms, to be proposed in this book as providing together the only firm ground for the mind, its only possible liberation from mere fashion and hunch and opinion, and therefore the only possible basis for a truly liberal education. The first of these was a basic realism, a basic rationlism too. The mind can in fact grasp reality—the reality of pigs and ducks, for example; it is not tied down to endless self-doubt, or to the treadmill of fashion and subjectivism. And reasoning is valid: sentences or statements or predications can sometimes be ascertainably true or false.

So much will perhaps be conceded. But I now want to propose a second and more controversial dogma; and even if I have succeeded in drawing that word's sting, even if I have anticipated and partly inhibited the knee-jerk response of hostility which it elicits so widely in a sceptical society, I shall still be stamping on certain toes, and also raising questions which go far beyond the scope of this book.

Let us suppose that we are casting about for something like an achieved wisdom, an achieved certainty as regards the ultimates. As free men, we are concerned with ends rather than means, with the nature and purpose of human existence; and we know that in all such matters, opinions and scepticisms are ten-a-penny. But is there anybody who even claims to *know*? And how plausibly?

The first of those two questions can (I suggest) be answered quite easily. In the present-day world, there are only two solid dogmatisms, only two major bodies of opinion which in fact claim to offer something more than mere opinion and are taken seriously by very large numbers of very intelligent people. (They have numerous competitors: I intend no offence when I say that these tend to be small, or local, or temporary, or clearly eccentric or irrational in nature.)

Of these two great universal dogmatisms, these two major options, the first is Marxism, especially in its fully-developed Communist version; and the second is Christianity, especially in its fully-developed Roman Catholic version. Each certainly claims to know the answers. But how plausibly?

The case for and against each of these two creeds has of course been argued already, very widely and very thoroughly, and I do not propose to recapitulate those arguments here. But while I have practically no personal sympathy or agreement with Marxism, I want to give credit where credit is due; and it seems to me that if you take a *low* view of liberal education, we have to regard it as something that flourishes excellently in Communist societies. (My prejudices are such that I regard this as an excellent *a priori* reason for distrusting that low view of liberal education.) Those societies are certainly tyrannical in a host of senses—social, economic, political, and philosophico-religious above all. But in their paternalistic and controlling way, they devote great efforts and resources to the leisure-time development of mind and body. This becomes internationally conspicuous in the field of sport: the Western athlete finds himself up against a Soviet competitor who lives as a privileged citizen, an aristocrat almost, backed up by all the training and equipment and general help and encouragement which a chauvinistic State can provide. And something similar is true of the arts. 'Socialist realism' in painting is something of a joke. Even so, in the Soviet Union and within its empire, the artist and the poet and the novelist and the musician are regarded as very important people, to be honoured and encouraged by the community, so long as they toe the Party line and give no trouble. In present-day England, the fact that I'm a writer subjects me to certain government penalties: in the Soviet Union—so long as I toed the line—it would gain for me a number of government privileges. And Moscow remains just about the best city in the world for the lover of ballet.

If liberal education is to be understood in a primarily cultural sense (which is, perhaps, how most people understand it in the West), the Marxist can at least make a plausible claim to be its friend. He has his dogmatism about the ultimates. But subject to that dogmatism, he favours a full cultural development of the mind by the educational process, just as he favours a full development of the body on the playing field and the athletic track. This is excellent as far as it goes.

But it doesn't go very far; and to claim that it offers 'liberation' in any really deep sense would be a sick joke. It is probably true that in certain Communist countries, the mass of the people are better fed today than at any time in their past—though this is the result of twentieth-century technology in general, and has been achieved in spite of Communist ideology rather than because of it. But a very heavy price is paid in terms of freedom—of political freedom, and also of intellectual freedom. Those countries are run on a basis closely analogous to slavery; and it may be useful to remember that where actual slavery has prevailed, it has often been in the owner's interest to keep his human property well-fed and reasonably contented.

Marxist Communism certainly claims to know the answers —to be the final solution to the human problem. But if we are thinking of truth and freedom—and, in particular, of the principle that "the truth shall make you free"—this claim lacks all credibility. Its dogmatic basis is (in my view) preposterous, being rooted in certain outstandingly callow manifestations of nineteenth-century muddle-headedness: in the last resort it is self-contradictory, since you cannot claim that your ideology is 'true' while at the same time declaring objective truth to be among the fallacies of bourgeois idealism.

If we are searching for an all-embracing world-view to serve as a basic wisdom, and therefore as the basis for liberal education, then Marxism will have to be rejected—not because it is dogmatic, but because it is erroneously dogmatic.

It is my belief that the Christian faith of the Roman Catholic Church is true; that it therefore offers the only real liberation of which humanity is capable; and that it also offers powerful support to the basic realism and rationalism which was my first dogma. This is my second; and I take it to be the only sound basis for a genuinely liberal education today, just as it led to the full flowering of liberal education in the past.

This is not a work of apologetics, and I do not intend to embark here upon any defence or justification of these assertions. But they can do with a little amplification.

It needs to be stressed, first of all, that the Church offers its 'Catholic' or universal Faith to mankind as being *true*. This might seem too obvious to need saying. But in our sceptical time, there is such a widespread dislike of dogmatism—of certainty and final conclusions in any ultimate matter at all—that the Church's central claim is constantly being evaded or watered down. Some maintain that no question of truth of falsity arises in connection with doctrinal statements: these (they say) are merely verbalizations of religious experience, valid for those concerned, interesting for others, but equally misinterpreted by the man who asserts them as truth and the man who denies them as falsehood. Others, certain Catholics included, want the Faith to be a suggestion, a point of view, a process of enquiry, anything rather than a blunt assertion: they want it to be offered to mankind as being congenial, or comforting, or relevant to modern problems of the political and social kind, or 'meaningful' in some sense which implies a strong appeal to twentieth-century imaginations. Such people are right in what they assert but wrong in what they deny, and they confuse the issue. In particular cases, the Faith quite often does confer those side-benefits and others. But this is by accident: they are not (so to speak) in the contract, they are not the main point. What the Church primarily offers is the objective way and truth and life of Christ; and in our present context of education, our emphasis must be upon truth—upon truth which is actually known, as distinct from even the most august and probable of opinions.

It is often pointed out that 'faith' is something more than an outward assent to doctrinal propositions. It is indeed. But it's something *more* than that, not something less. It needs blood and a heart; but if it's to stand up, it also needs a bone-structure of intellectually apprehended truth. And since the truth in question comes from God and not from man, it is apprehended with a unique *kind* of certainty, not paralleled in any other operation of the intellect, but fully defensible by those other operations—logical, historical, scientific, and so forth—within the limits of their terms of reference. Transcending all such human and academic methods but making good use of them, and not at any point denying their autonomy or otherwise making enemies of them, the Church asserts that certain things are in fact the case, that certain doctrinal and moral propositions are in fact true and that to deny them is to utter falsehood. Faith doesn't finish there, but it does begin there.

In view of that present-day dislike of all such dogmatism, it may be as well to point out here that there is absolutely no arrogance in this claim to offer certain truth as against human opinion. Particular Popes and bishops and theologians have of course been arrogant in their personal behaviour from time to time: they are only human, and they have their failings like the rest of us. But their dogmatic inflexibility in asserting Catholic truth was never based upon any arrogant confidence in their own powers, their own superior wisdom. In the intellectual and academic world generally, we often find that the general scepticism already mentioned co-exists with particular dogmatism which might indeed be considered arrogant: things are said which carry the implied rubric "We know the answers, because we are extremely clever people and have studied this subject very thoroughly". (There are certain Catholic theologians today who dogmatise freely on the basis of just such a self-conferred *magisterium*.) But the implied rubric of the Church's doctrinal assertions is quite different and very much more humble: "This is the message which we were told to pass on to you."

Theologically speaking, the Papacy and the teaching Church in general have to be considered in very lofty terms. But the corresponding human behaviour is not like that of the proud man who thinks himself wiser than everybody else: it is much more like the humble function of the letter-carrier or messenger-boy.

The message so passed on to us is one of liberation. Christ sets us free from sin, from the taking of false turnings in life, which is why he is called 'the way'; he sets us free from ignorance and scepticism, from the existential anguish of bewilderment in a meaningless universe, which is why he is called 'the truth'; and he sets us free from the dreadful finality of death, which is why he is called 'the life'. Once again, in this educational context, it is truth that we emphasize; and it is one prime consequence of Catholic truth that we can speak with well-justified confidence about those ultimate questions which concern us as free men.

It is a negative statement of the case, perhaps, which will make this privilege most apparent. Suppose that Catholicism is not true, or has not yet reached us. A servile education can still be acquired, and may lead to great technical and economic achievements: cultural activities may still palliate the essential slavery of our condition, and may be splendidly creative. But beyond these things we shall be in the dark. We shall face the pagan's bewilderment, his ultimate despair: there will be hints, dreams, myths, suggestions, but we shall *know* nothing about the meaning and purpose of the universe or about our own nature and destiny. We shall be enslaved to ultimate meaninglessness, adrift in the dark upon uncharted seas.

In providing firm ground beneath our feet, in giving us knowledge—otherwise unavailable—of what we are and where we are going and why, Catholicism makes possible the distinctive use of the intellect which characterizes the free man. Without it, liberal education—however rich and rewarding in peripheral ways—is bound to be sterile and dead at the centre.

Here, at this Californian college, I have spoken to many students who have encountered that central sterility and deadness on other campuses. Their delighted relief at liberation from it has gladdened my soft parental heart.

Then, beyond truth and the consequent liberation, I would make a third and rather pragmatic claim for the Catholic Faith. As my prime dogma, I offered a certain basic realism and rationalism. Pigs are indeed pigs and ducks are indeed ducks: reality is indeed real and can be apprehended by the mind: reason is indeed valid and can achieve solid results when properly used. This might be called the common-sense of the ordinary man.

But it is a common-sense to which some people can only cling with difficulty. The young couple whom I mentioned earlier had been indoctrinated with the idea that they ought to doubt and question everything forever, including their own eyes and their own minds: they also lived (like so many) under the peculiar stresses of a fragmented and collapsing society. If they were in a thoroughly confused state, it was understandable: teachers and circumstances alike had long been pushing them in what I would call a rather nutty direction.

But such particular explanations are insufficient. The denial of reason and reality is no local and temporary phenomenon of today's troubled West: whole civilizations, whole religions of great depth and subtlety have been built upon the belief that all perceived phenoma are *maya* or illusion, that all deep truth has to be self-contradictory. Even where reality is conceded to the visible universe, it is often regarded as an evil sort of reality, its creator having some more or less Satanic character: sensitive minds have always been vexed by the problem of evil, and various versions of the Gnostic or Manichaean answer to that problem have been accepted and welcomed by people of different countries and cultures at many periods—especially, as Jean Guitton observed, at times of particular stress.

It is (I suggest) a kind of basic sanity to trust one's own senses and one's own reasoning powers within obvious limitations, and also to recognize a certain ontological goodness in being as such, a trustworthiness in the universe. But any such basic sanity is easily lost, what with the stress of experience in this life; and it is directly assaulted by such religions and philosophies as are negativistic and sceptical.

It is directly and powerfully supported, however, by Catholicism—which, in so far as it is both understood and lived, makes philosophical and psychological sense of the universe and safeguards that precarious faith in common-sense and reason and goodness, though with full recognition of the limitations and dangers and difficulties.

This is not the greatest benefit conferred by the Faith, but it is a considerable one, highly relevant to the problems of those who hope to offer a liberal education to young people at a time of notable stress. The recognition that pigs are pigs and that ducks are ducks is (in one sense) a brisk non-controversial starting-point for the whole religious and philosophical enquiry. But in another and all too topical sense, it can become a saving but mysterious dogma, desperately urged by the Church upon those who are sliding towards the pit of insanity.

It is a matter of fairly common observation that the Catholic Faith, when devoutly and meditatively lived, is in itself a very real education. I myself have known people who, after only a rudimentary schooling, have been mentally ripened by that Faith (and usually by suffering as well) into a kind of wisdom very much like what you find in the best kind of scholar. One can sometimes come across an extreme case, in which the person concerned might be called 'a great philosopher' without any undue straining of language.

But there would always be *some* straining of language. In my view, the acceptance and devout living of the Catholic Faith has an importance which makes all other considerations—educational considerations, for example—seem relatively trivial. None the less, at their own level, such considerations do have their importance. The Faith alone can educate you, make you (perhaps) into a great philosopher. But there is also a case for being educated, and for becoming a philosopher or lover of wisdom, in the more obvious and conventional senses of those words. The two possibilities are in no kind of conflict.

In other words, while we need religion first of all, we also need theology. I have just been suggesting that Catholicism is the necessary basis of any fully 'liberal' education: this is not its prime function, but is among its good secondary functions. But to perform this educational function satisfactorily, it will need a degree of intellectual systematisation: it will need to be thought out, in a way which we find clearly foreshadowed in the New Testament and the life of the early Church, but which took some time to reach any full development. And beyond this, it will need a fully-worked-out relationship to philosophy and—through philosophy—to all the various fields and disciplines which concern the student and his teachers.

This is a secondary kind of requirement: the Church existed for well over a thousand years without having any clear-cut way of meeting it. But it was met in due course.

I must therefore supplement my two main dogmatisms with a third. I have already said that if there is to be any genuinely 'liberal' education, it will necessarily be based upon the Catholic Faith. I now want to say that it will be extremely well advised to base itself upon that Faith as systematized in the philosophy and theology of St Thomas Aquinas.

That distinction, between necessity and wise counsel, is important. It is not, in the last analysis, essential to be a Thomist if one hopes to be a Catholic. That whole millennium of Catholics lived and died and went to their reward without ever having heard of Thomism; and from the start, the Church has allowed and encouraged a degree of philosophical and theological pluralism, so that a Franciscan (for example) can now receive his whole formation within a tradition which, although fully Catholic, is notably not Thomistic. The rightness of St Thomas is not *de fide*: a Catholic, as such, is not committed to it.

None the less, the Church in her wisdom has gone remarkably far towards imposing such a commitment. She has never *quite* said that Thomism is part of the deposit of Faith, which wouldn't be true. But she seems to me to have gone as close to that assertion as was theologically possible.

One can ask whether this was wise and proper. Does philosophy—when strictly so called, and distinguished most carefully from theology—lie within the competence of the Church?

Well, it certainly lies within the competence of suitable

churchmen; and while there are certain fine points to be made here, it seems to me clear that this was a wise policy. I have three rather non-theological reasons for thinking so.

In the first place, St Thomas is pre-eminently the philosopher of common-sense. All the other great philosophers, from Descartes at least, have started off by asking us to believe something which is (on the face of it) ridiculous: as, that there is no such thing as matter; or, that there is nothing except matter; or, that you have no sure knowledge of anything except yourself; or, that you have no free will. From such starting-points, they go on and say various clever things. But an air of unreality, even of quiet lunacy, pervades the whole of what they say. St Thomas at least has his feet on the good democratic ground of human common-sense—on the principle, if you like, that the True Light enlightens *every* man born into this world, not only the rarefied clevers. There are optical illusions: you and I can be deceived: we can make mistakes. But St Thomas has a most refreshing belief that the world is really there, and is more or less as we see it: also, that we can say true things about it, and draw conclusions, and reach certainties with safety.

He is not a particularly easy author to read. None the less, when we turn to him from most philosophy of the post-Cartesian sort, it's like re-joining the human race: it's like waking up from a nightmare. It should be clear to my readers by now that the nightmare in question, and the process of waking up or escaping from it, is the principal subject of this book.

Then, in the second place, St Thomas is pre-eminently the philosopher of the goodness of being: the remedy, therefore, for the currently epidemic plague of quasi-Manichaean distrust and denial and consequent despair. I have already quoted from Chesterton's book about him: a profound book but an entertaining one too, since the two men were so totally alike in some respects and so ludicrously unlike in others. But Chesterton—no philosopher himself—did grasp the point of St Thomas, and chiefly (I think) because he himself had been through that private Hell of distrust and denial and despair. "Nobody will begin to understand the Thomist philosophy, or indeed the Catholic philosophy, who does not realize that the primary and fundamental part of it is entirely the praise of Life; the praise of

Being; the praise of God as Creator of the world. Everything else follows a long way after that, being conditioned by various complications like the Fall or the vocation of heroes." And: "If the morbid Renaissance intellectual is supposed to say 'To be or not to be—that is the question', then the massive mediaeval doctor does most certainly reply in a voice of thunder 'To be—that is the answer'."

An answer apt and topical for many people—for abortionists and population-controllers, for example, and certainly for tortured students. St Thomas puts his finger on the point at which the campus suicide-rate originates.

Let me approach his pre-eminence from a third and slightly different angle. Many people, by no means all of them Catholics, are perturbed because modern Western society seems to have lost contact with something which may seem rather undefinable —with its origins, perhaps, or its great tradition. Not everybody will equate this with the Catholic Faith; and in all sorts of cultural and philosophical and educational senses, it is something historically associated with that Faith but distinct from it. But the problem of putting this into words is a tricky one: it may be present to our minds as little more than a vague nostalgia, a feeling that the modern world took a terribly wrong turning somewhere without quite noticing that it was doing so, so that the present-day West is much more disoriented and unhappy and underconfident than it ever needed to be, unnecessarily vulnerable therefore before the barbarians, whom most of us will equate with the plainly dynamic power of Communism. We have lost something, but what? Let us call it a certain civilization, with Hebraic and Greek and Roman origins, and incorporating some elements from further afield; and my point is that this also has its philosopher. "I am convinced", says Dr Josef Pieper, "that Thomas Aquinas, by virtue of his truly creative selflessness, has had the power to bring the whole contrapuntal diversity of these very different strands of tradition into an intellectual order, without any omissions and without any systematising violence. It is certainly a task that calls of course for an enormous power of assimilation and a power of clarification amounting to genius."

If you feel nostalgic and protective about something which

might loosely be called 'the Western tradition', anxious to save it and pass it on to the young in some form that will stand up to the most rigorous intellectual battering, then St Thomas is your man —even if you are not yourself a Catholic. He knew that there are things more important than education and civilization. But precisely for that reason, he remains the greatest of all merely human educators, the greatest of all merely human civilizers.

Chapter VII:
THE WORD 'CATHOLIC'

I stayed up late last night, discussing all things with half-a-dozen of the students. One thing at least hasn't changed since my own student days at Oxford: the later it gets, the more profound and universal the subject under discussion becomes. At nine, perhaps, you're discussing politics, in the form of some currently newsworthy piece of public villainy: by ten, you've got to the principles of political action; by eleven, to the general principles of all human action, and by twelve, to the nature of the good and the beautiful and the true. Before the party breaks up in the small hours, God himself will have been given the full treatment. And last night, we didn't start with politics.

Now, while the morning sunlight lifts a light frost off the rolling parkland, I raise my eyes to the encircling mountains, which remind me of the ones that overhang El Escorial in Spain; and I reflect upon the light which last night's discussion casts upon the rather exceptional character of this college.

To start with, it is naturally a Catholic college. I have already suggested that liberal education must of necessity be religious: that is to say, it earns its title by being concerned with ends rather than with means, with the great ultimates primarily, and then with particulars in relation to them. I have also suggested that it needs to be dogmatic, and for two complementary reasons. Subjectively speaking, psychologically speaking, young people need to be given assurance and a feeling of certainty, to be liberated from the prison-like experience of scepticism. But the assurance and certainty in question need to be objectively valid, to be *true*. Such organizations as the *Hitler-Jugend* of Nazi Germany and the 'Young Communists' League' of present-day

Russia have succeeded in liberating their members from the feeling of uncertainty, giving them a fine sense of dogmatic assurance instead; but that assurance has in each case been erroneous, conferring no real liberation at all—objectively speaking—but only a new imprisonment in evil fantasy.

From the truth of the Catholic Faith (which, for the purposes of this book, I am treating as a premise or datum), it follows that liberal education can only reach its true fulfilment in a Catholic college. But in this age of ecumenism, I would qualify that statement by saying that it can reach a fair degree of fulfilment in (say) a Protestant or Jewish college. In the subjective sense mentioned above, it can do so in so far as the life and work of the college is based upon strong religious convictions; in the more objective sense, it can do so in so far as those convictions are in fact true and adequate. Each of these conditions is partially met by a great many such institutions, but always—in my experience—with some kind of built-in limitation. I am thinking in particular of certain Protestant colleges of the 'fundamentalist' kind, within which the idea of a liberal education is pursued most nobly and not without success, but suffers radical frustration or semi-schizophrenia because of an underlying anti-intellectualism in religious matters.

But if all this be agreed, we have still arrived only at the familiar notion of a Catholic college—one which will use the mind of St Thomas as a primary educational instrument. Aren't there a great many such colleges, in the United States and elsewhere? What's so special about this place? If I have fallen in love with it, could this be a kind of random infatuation, arising from my experience of particularly pleasant company in particularly pleasant surroundings?

One thing is clear: it can't be the kind of infatuation for which we blame the demon drink. I am not seeing the college through any golden haze of martini-fumes: it shares with the U.S. Navy the hideous fault of being 'dry'.

That, I think, is the worst thing I can say about it.

There are certainly a great many Catholic colleges in the United States, some with full university standing, some with the different standing of the Liberal Arts College. Comparable institutions exist in most parts of the world. We don't have them in England, but this is because we have proportionately fewer Catholics and an educational system which is structured on different lines throughout.

Even so, every such assertion needs to be qualified. It needs to be said that not all supposedly 'Catholic' institutions really deserve the name.

This is not the place for any full analysis of present-day religious controversy, and I do not wish to be more judgmental than the nature of my subject dictates. Let me therefore approach the matter in semantic rather than theological terms, and consider how that word 'Catholic' can most properly and accurately be used.

Language can only be an effective instrument of communication if words are used in their common and public senses. There are many technical and specialized words, of course, which the layman will understand imperfectly or not at all; but as between the specialists who use them, such words are common ground, having their definable and agreed meanings. In so far as this ceases to be true, communication becomes impossible. If I use a word in one sense and you understand it in another, we shall be at cross-purposes: our discussion will get nowhere at all.

In the small matters of daily life, such cross-purposes are constantly arising, and can usually be resolved by a little explanation. They can often be amusing: in particular, ludicrous misunderstandings can arise from the differences between American and English usage. An effect of gross indecency is sometimes given where none was intended. I could tell you many anecdotes about all this, some of them fit for polite company, some of them rather less so.

All this is good fun and gives much scope for word-games. But in so far as any matter is important, such misunderstandings matter: they need to be avoided, if necessary by much careful definition of terms. And since this cannot always be done, it is an important part of intellectual responsibility to use words in their public and generally-accepted senses as far as possible, with full explanation when this is not possible. To use any important word in some Pickwickian or Humpty-Dumpty-ish sense of your own—without saying that you're doing so—is to darken counsel and generate confusion.

Now the word 'Catholic', as adjective or noun, has a public and generally-understood sense which is quite clear, and within which there are two elements. The first is juridical or canonical: it concerns an individual's formal relationship to one visible institution, distinguishing him from an apostate or one who has been excommunicated. With this slightly specialized sense of the word, I shall not be concerned further. Its much more common usage refers to an individual's belief; and here, it refers primarily to his acceptance of a certain authority, as teaching with the voice of God and not of man.

The heart of the word's meaning lies there. Many theological subtleties are of course involved. Certain Catholics in the past have needed to be reminded that 'the teaching of the Church' is not the same thing as 'the opinions currently dominant among ecclesiastics': many Catholics today need to be reminded that it isn't the same thing as 'the ideas currently fashionable among those members of the intelligentsia who choose to call themselves Catholics'. The term is an objective one, misused by each of these two groups. It does not refer to any merely coincidental agreement with the teaching Church: it is antithetical to any notion of the individual reaching his own conclusions and then accepting the Church in the measure of its agreement with himself. Nor can it, without logical absurdity, be selective: you cannot say with one breath "I believe that the Catholic Church teaches with the voice of God" and with the next "But I can't go along with the Catholic Church when it teaches so-and-so". The traditional name for such selectivity is *hairesis* or 'heresy', which *means* selectivity and is the word most clearly antithetical to 'Catholic'.

I am making a semantic point, not a theological one: all the above is an approach to what the word 'Catholic' means in its public and accepted sense, whether an atheist or a believer is speaking.

Here is another such approach. It is an abuse of language to call anything 'Catholicism'—with approval or with disapproval—unless it's recognisably the same thing as the religion to which Newman was converted, which St Thomas explored so profoundly, which St Augustine brought to Canterbury, which the apostles preached after the first Pentecost—a religion which 'developed' (in Newman's slightly technical sense) over that long period but did not change otherwise. It is logically possible for a man to consider that religion false and so to repudiate it; and it is important to note that he will be doing exactly this—in principle—if he denies the clearly defined teaching of the Church at *any* point. He may still agree with the Church about everything else. But his agreement will now be of the coincidental or selective kind: he will have rejected the central idea that defines Catholicism as against some vague and generalised Christianity, the idea that the Church (which is not to be confused with the churchmen within it) speaks with the voice of God. And he cannot by-pass this problem by invoking some notion of a liberalised, freely-evolving Catholicism, wholly at liberty to repudiate its own past and come up with radically new ideas, but still entitled to call itself by the old name. That's the Humpty-Dumpty method, and it only generates confusion: some part of what the word 'Catholicism' *means* is a firm rejection of all such thinking, a firm commitment to the particular Faith that comes to us from the Apostles.

It would be possible to say, erroneously (in my view) but without semantic confusion, that Catholicism has now been found untrue and that a new religion has therefore been developed to take its place, having within it certain elements or memories of Catholicism. But whether we accept it or not, this new thing should be given a new name. If we attach the old label to a radically different product, we shall only generate confusion.

Much confusion of that kind is in fact generated nowadays, by people who still insist on calling themselves 'Catholics' in some private or Pickwickian sense of that word, when its public and accepted sense has plainly ceased to be applicable to them. One can only guess at their motives for thus torturing the language: most of us are fairly straightforward in proclaiming our beliefs and loyalties and in desiring these to be correctly labelled, and to be re-labelled if they change. Imagine some man who used to be a convinced Communist. He now decides that Marx and Lenin were fools, that dialectical materialism is a heap of old nonsense, that economic life needs to be based upon the free market and the profit-motive, and that the best government is a theocratic monarchy. Will he then continue to call himself a Communist, explaining (if you ask him) that his Communism is of the new, up-dated, progressive kind? Probably not—though the case of Dr Ota Sik, a distinguished Czecho-Slovak economist and Deputy Prime Minister who left his country when the Russians came in 1968, suggests that in some changes of allegiance at least, a man can indeed go through a period of trying to have it both ways.

It's hard to be wholly rational, wholly consistent: it's painful to break with old loyalties, old sentiments, old friends, old habits.

There is nothing secret about the fact that the Catholic scene is a rather troubled one nowadays, notably in Holland and France and Canada and the United States, and especially where the intelligentsia are concerned, clerical and lay. Over the last few years, many such people, while anxious to remain Catholics in the juridical sense already mentioned, have formed a steady and consistent habit of saying things which make it clear that they are *not* Catholics by belief. They have lost the Faith—temporarily, we hope—and are unable or unwilling to face the fact of their loss.

This would doubtlessly be regarded—by them—as an unfair and rather offensive statement of the case. "No, we haven't 'lost the Faith'. We've recovered it: that is, we've liberated the Church from an old legalistic stagnation and literalism, giving it a new and dynamic kind of life, a new relevance for the future. Ours is the real Catholicism of today."

Claims of more or less that kind are often made nowadays, by people who are saying things wholly incompatible with anything that 'Catholicism' has ever meant before. They are not made realistically: what thus claims to be the mainstream is very manifestly proving to be a stagnant backwater. But I do find them entertaining: they have the pleasant absurdity which characterizes a whole class of relativistic inversions. A humourist, describing a personal difference of opinion, once said: "I then struck him savagely on the fist with the point of my chin." In very much the same way, when I stand on my head (as I often do) I can claim to be doing what Atlas did when he bore the whole world on his shoulders. Anything *can* be described in back-to-front language. There was once a comic history-book which said, in connection with the English Reformation, "the Pope and all his followers then seceded from the Church of England."

In just that way, we might say that in the course of these last few years, the Pope and the whole Universal Church have seceded from a small number of restless and querulous intellectuals.

But except when we are being unmistakeably frivolous, semantic and intellectual responsibility dictates a more precise use of language. If some view is advanced which entails, as its logical consequence, the idea that the Catholic Church has radically misunderstood the Christian religion for nearly twenty centuries, its own nature and purpose included, then we can debate that view on its historical and theological merits. What we cannot do, if we have any respect for language, is to call the man who maintains it 'a Catholic' except in some purely juridical sense. Some kind of personal nostalgia may make him anxious to retain that title: in all charity and gentleness, we must detach him from it—not because the Pope says so, but because the dictionary says so.

If truth matters, then the communication of truth matters; and it then becomes very important to use words accurately. If any man wants to say that Catholicism is untrue, let him do so. But let us defend the poor battered old language against those who use words in private Pickwickian senses of their own—and in particular, against the man who does this because he's desperate to find some way of being a Catholic without actually being a Catholic.

It isn't only individuals who do this: it's institutions as well, especially educational institutions, since teachers and other intellectuals are the people chiefly at risk in this respect. Hence, while it is easy to find something which is *called* a Catholic college, it has now become distinctly difficult to find a college which can be *accurately* so labelled.

What considerations govern the accurate use of that adjective, as applied to academic institutions rather than to individual people?

Let it be agreed, at the outset, that an educated man needs to know something about Catholicism. This necessity has nothing to do with belief. Even an atheist, if he is totally ignorant of the Faith and how it hangs together and how it works, will find this ignorance a serious handicap when he embarks upon the study of—say—history and literature and art. In just the same sense, I would say that an educated Catholic should know at least something about Hinduism and Islam: also, that a responsible citizen nowadays needs to know at least the rudiments of Marxism. The list of such necessities could be extended.

Whether by courses of formal instruction or otherwise, a good liberal education will therefore teach you something *about* Catholicism, something *about* Hinduism and Islam, something *about* Marxism, and so forth. But this is quite different from *teaching* you Catholicism, from *teaching* you Hinduism or Islam, from *teaching* you Marxism. The Communists are well aware of the difference. In the schools and colleges of the Soviet Union, Marxism is not offered to the students as an intellectual option and a subject about which one needs to be well-informed: it is offered to them as the way, the truth, and the life. Thus we can speak of a Marxist education, as against one that merely educates about Marxism.

A Catholic education, and therefore a Catholic college, can be defined on the same lines. It will naturally cause the student to become better informed about his Faith than he was. But even this important task will be—in a certain sense—secondary: it will be a kind of by-product of his education *in* the Faith, in the way and truth and life of Christ, by an academic community which is wholly committed *to* that Faith, to that way and truth and life. The institution will define itself by that commitment: in any suggestion that Catholicism is one intellectual option among many, one coherent and plausible set of opinions to be recommended for the student's consideration, it will recognize a direct challenge to its own nature and purpose and indeed to any real possibility of a liberal education. Such thought leads us straight back to the unhappy jailhouse of relativistic scepticism.

Theology, in a college which can fully and accurately be called 'Catholic', will therefore hold a position which will be unique in various distinct ways.

In various practical and daily senses, it will of course be one 'subject' among others, to be studied at certain times according to a set syllabus; and for obvious religious reasons, it will be regarded as the most important subject of all. But apart from this, at the merely human level, it will be given a magisterial or sapiential primacy over all other subjects.

The practical value of this is sometimes overlooked. The fact is that in many secular fields, the Catholic student has an unfair advantage over every other kind of student: he has a touchstone of truth, by which a wide variety of new theories and opinions can be given at least a time-saving provisional evaluation. Let us imagine the announcement of some new doctrine in (say) psychology or sociology. The Catholic student considers this and finds that it fits in beautifully with what the Church has been saying for two millennia: he knows at once that it's going to be worth serious consideration and may well prove a major advancement of knowledge. But perhaps he considers it and finds that it clashes violently with the Church's teaching, is quite incompatible with Catholicism: in this case, while he may decide to keep an eye on the new doctrine and follow its development for controversial reasons, he knows that in itself it is not going to be worth serious consideration. It's going to be one of the numerous blind alleys or dead ends which litter the history of thought.

Such judgments need to be made cautiously, especially by young people who don't know quite as much as they think they do: the compatibility *or* the incompatibility of this new doctrine with Catholicism may be less total and obvious than a hasty mind supposes. Even so, a fully Catholic college will make sure that the student gets the full benefit of that unfair advantage conferred by his Faith.

It will also take care not to compartmentalize his mind. If it treats the Faith as a kind of extra, as something added to an education which—in secular subjects—is exactly the same as that offered by secular colleges, stress or conflict is going to arise in the student's mind, and this will be intellectually improper and psychologically disastrous.

The scope of such dangers is not always recognized. English Catholics have long been aware of the anti-Catholic bias cherished—not always consciously—by many historians: I was brought up to be on my guard in this respect. But there are many other fields in which, less obviously and therefore more dangerously, prevailing beliefs are governed by the secular and positivistic assumptions of most present-day society. Even the natural sciences are not immune from this tendency. Observable facts are observable facts. But the selection and arrangement and interpretation of observable facts, and the placing of emphasis here or there, will always be influenced—again, perhaps unconsciously—by the mental 'set' of those who do the work. This becomes clearly apparent in books about the origin of the world, or of life, or of man. Such a book will set forth the factual evidence honestly enough. But it will sometimes set this forth as seen by a man who is very strongly motivated to show, or to suggest, that the 'hypothesis' of God is not going to be necessary after all; that things can be somehow explained without Him. One hesitates to accuse scientific writers of such philosophical innocence: unfortunately, they often leave one with no option. An ill-informed bias is plainly present, and it mars the objectivity of the book.

Such a bias can affect many subjects, and invisibly except to highly-trained minds. Hence, a situation can arise in which while theology classes are conducted on the premise that Catholicism is true, the study of most other subjects is vitiated by a million tiny imperceptible suggestions that Catholicism is *not* true. The practical danger is that the student's mind may become split: he is likely to end up with a vague feeling that 'religious truth' and 'scientific truth' are unrelated or perhaps in conflict, and even that a certain belief can be true in religion but not in science. For St Thomas Aquinas, this kind of intellectual schizophrenia—as personfied by Siger of Brabant—was a kind of ultimate enemy. For him, it was a sin against the integrity of the mind: we, in this generation, will also see the psychological dangers involved.

A fully Catholic college, teaching in the spirit of St Thomas, will avoid this danger instinctively. It will not merely grant to theology a primacy of honour and a magisterial or corrective function: it will act on the principle that philosophy and theology are logically anterior to all other studies, are the basis which they must presuppose and the only frame of reference within which they can fruitfully exist. It will see all truth as one, and will provide the student with well-tested machinery with which he can resolve apparent discrepancies or contradictions within it.

It will go further. I have already mentioned the fact that the Catholic religion, when fully and meditatively lived, is in itself a kind of education and a good one. A truly Catholic college will of course act on this principle. But it will also act on the converse principle.

The Faith, it it's anything at all, has to be the central and most important thing in life: it cannot—without absurdity and indeed sin—be compartmentalized off into a kind of spare-time hobby, a specialized interest and activity for Sunday mornings. All life is a service and seeking of God, or should be; and this goes pre-eminently for the academic and intellectual life, since this is a service and seeking of truth, and 'Truth' is one of the names of God.

It follows that while religion is educative, education itself should be a primarily religious activity, a mode of worship, and not only when its contents is explicitly theological. This will be the background assumption, the background motivation of *all* activities within a fully Catholic college. They are all God-oriented, though some are oriented towards God in Himself and some towards God in His human and other creation.

Consider astronomy, for example. Of this as of many other studies, we can say what was once said splendidly of Greek literature, that it "not only elevates above the vulgar herd, but leads not infrequently to positions of considerable emolument". The student can be pardoned if some part of him thinks along those lines: he has his way to make in the world, after all. But the whole atmosphere and climate of a truly Catholic college will steadily pressure him to see astronomy in different and higher terms—as something which finds its charter and its ultimate point in that joyous shout of the Psalmist, *Caeli enarrant gloriam Dei, et opera manuum eius annuntiat firmamentum*—The heavens declare the glory of God, and the firmament proclaims His handiwork.

So with all studies; and indeed, so with collegiate life in general. The old English notion of what college was, at Oxford and Cambridge, centered around the idea of a chapel for common worship, a library for common study, and a hall for common living—the three forming an architectural and social unity, primarily religious in function, so that the visiting tourist can now see the whole thing as a kind of extended church.

On that same principle, in a fully Catholic college of this age, a student should be able to go from morning Mass to the dining-hall for a talkative meal with his friends, and from there to the library or the physics laboratory, without any feeling that the subject was (so to speak) changed at any point in this progression.

The subject, throughout, was God.

In this age of social fragmentation and consequent loneliness, I would myself lay great emphasis upon the Catholic college as a place of 'togetherness', of experienced Christian community, of love; and for this reason I would want it to be small, a family rather than a crowd. But I would lay much greater emphasis upon that concept of education as a primarily religious activity, a mode of worship, unified by having that character and purpose at every point. I would even go so far as to regret the existence of chaplains, specialized as such. A certain priestly presence is of course needed. But the distinctive office of the chaplain does suggest that religion is a kind of department, separate from the rest of life and needing its own management. I may be hyper-sensitive here; but it seems to me that any such suggestion opens the way to a basic fragmentation—to the too-familiar situation in which unrelated studies are chosen at random and with no overall guiding principle, with 'religion' available among them if your tastes point that way.

These, I suggest, are the considerations which need to be borne in mind if we are to talk accurately about 'a Catholic college', as against a college in which there happen to be some Catholics.

But the most important of all such considerations, of course, is that the adjective should be fully and precisely applicable to the individuals concerned, and above all to the faculty, by the standards mentioned earlier. I am not suggesting that there is no place at all in the Catholic college for the Protestant or Jewish instructor, or even the atheist, so long as he is known and recognized to be such and is prepared to co-operate with the college's distinctive purpose. The disastrous thing would be the appointment of faculty-members who called themselves Catholics but were not in fact Catholic believers.

Such instructors are numerous today: as I have already observed, it is among educated people, among the intelligentsia, that there chiefly prevails the syndrome which can be summed up in the words "I am a Catholic, of course, but. . . ." People so afflicted should not be employed by the Catholic college, as instructors of the young, if it desires to go on deserving the adjective. Only those should be recruited who are fully committed to the actual Catholic Faith, as mediated to us by the actual *magisterium* of the actual Church—and a few, perhaps, who make no claim to be Catholics at all.

The principle here involved is a simple one: it is that in an institution devoted to the life of the intellect, integrity demands that things should be called by their proper names. Ships should sail under their own flags. When they refuse to do so, the principles of the academic community (as such) are violated, no less than the principles of the Catholic community.

As a necessary means of self-preservation, a Catholic college should therefore recruit its faculty-members and establish the conditions of their tenure on frankly-proclaimed principles which differ sharply from those prevailing elsewhere. Now and again—very seldom, we hope—it will terminate an appointment which a secular college would have continued.

Vehement but ill-considered feelings about 'academic freedom' have created a situation in which many people will react explosively to any such suggestion. The subject therefore needs a little development.

If a man holds paid office as a teacher of Catholic theology, his subject-matter is twofold. Initially, he is concerned with the important but rather limited field of natural theology—with the existence of God and the immortality of the soul, and with such other religious principles as can be known or suspected in the absence of a revelation. Beyond this, his subject-matter is the actual revelation of God, as mediated to us by the Church; and as we all know, good work in this field will not only educate the young, but will sometimes help the Church wonderfully in its necessary task of doctrinal development.

But like any other academic, he has to believe in his own subject-matter and respect its objective and determinate character. He may have his own reasons for wishing that the revelation of God were other than what it is: all of us find reality tiresome at times. But his job is to study that great reality in its determinate objectivity: he has no business to deny it, or to modify it, or to distort it. If he does any of these things, he is sinning against the academic code no less than against the Catholic code: he is comparable to the scientist who fakes the result of an unrepeatable experiment to support his pet theory, or the literary historian who secretly destroys some embarrassing document.

What, then if he reaches some personal conviction which is flatly incompatible with the Catholic Faith?

Ideally, it will dawn upon him that he may possibly be mistaken. If not, basic integrity demands that he should resign his office as a teacher of Catholic theology. He can of course take another title: he can call himself a teacher of comparative anthropology, or of social psychology, with special reference to the verbal and mental behaviour-patterns of Roman Catholics. He can talk about the Church from the outside. But from the premise which he has now accepted, it follows in logic that no revelation of God is in fact reliably mediated to man through the Church—in other words, that the subject which he has hitherto professed to teach does not really exist at all. It was never 'What men say about God', or even 'What the Church teaches about God': it was always 'God, as made known to us through the Church'. And since he now rejects the premise that God can be so known, he must not continue as teacher of a subject which is based upon that premise.

If the college or university or seminary therefore calls upon him to resign, it is guilty of no obscurantist tyranny: rather, it is living up to the autonomous principles of intellectual and linguistic integrity.

But with the few marginal exceptions already mentioned, *every* instructor in a fully Catholic college will be a teacher of Catholic theology, whether directly or indirectly. The appointment and tenure of each one will therefore be conditional upon the accuracy with which the word 'Catholic' can be applied to him, initially and throughout his teaching career.

If he has taken the point, he will not regard this as an arbitrary and cramping limitation: he will see it as a platitude, almost as a tautology. He will be at ease in this situation, and rightly so: if it irked him, he shouldn't be there at all.

It doesn't seem to irk anybody at this college; and when I look back at last night's discussion, I attribute some part of its quality to the fact that the word 'Catholic' is here used as the high-quality precision instrument which it is. I'm a logomaniac, a word-buff, and it breaks my heart to see how savagely some people handle it.

Chapter VIII:
THE SEVENFOLD WAY

A shocking thought occurred to me this afternoon: it was almost an indecency, and I'm not sure how to put it into words.

I had attended a couple of classes, and had lunch with the students, and afterwards I walked down to the lake with three of them and out to the broad leafy avenue. And all the time—as usual—my mind was at work on its problem of the moment: what *is* it that this particular college is doing for its young people?

The shocking thought which occurred to me under those trees was a partial answer: *the college is helping them to become ladies and gentlemen.* I blush to use such unfashionable language, but the fact is clear; and if my problem is that of trying to understand the sense of liberation which fills this air, I see here an important clue to it. I am here among people who have been let off one painful hook, people to whom one liberating message has been effectively given: *it is not actually compulsory to be a slob, a slattern, or a lout.*

An important message indeed, and it has nothing whatever to do with social snobbery. These students were not recruited from an elite: their acceptance by this college was not affected by any social, racial, sexual, or economic factors whatsoever. And the future that lies before them is (on the whole) unlikely to be of any aristocratic or privileged sort. Their minds are certainly being sharpened very efficiently, and this might qualify them to become 'great achievers': on the other hand, the wisdom in which they are being trained is such as to rule out any blind idolatry of money and 'success'.

It's in a different and deeper sense that they are now being helped to become ladies and gentlemen. I would state the matter, initially, in terms of courtesy and even of ceremony. These Catholic students cross themselves when they pass by the chapel: they are polite: their dress, though hardly formal by the standards of an Edwardian dinner-party, represents a bold challenge to the hair-and-dirt-and-shabbiness laws which are so slavishly obeyed elsewhere.

We should never despise Ceremony: the poet Chapman was right when he made that word into the name of a goddess, and represented that goddess as mankind's great defender against barbarism and ruin. All high civilizations have recognized this principle, and have attached great importance to formal or ritual or ordered behaviour, to good manners, to Ceremony. Their reasons for doing so have not been merely aesthetic. Man's image of himself is one of the great determinants of history; and between this and his behaviour-patterns, there is a two-way relationship of cause and effect. It is the instinct of all men and all societies to externalize and enact whatever notion they have of their own nature and destiny: conversely, our outward behaviour will always tend to modify the image of self and of society that we entertain. If in the secular culture of today most people tend to favour behaviour-patterns of the relaxed, casual, 'authentic', spontaneous, and slovenly kind, they thereby express *and reinforce* the very low view of man and of human destiny which characterizes that culture.

Here, I find an exactly similar two-way process at work, but in the opposite sense. In an atmosphere which some might expect to be restrictive, in however good a cause, I find instead a kind of liberation, and exaltation and flowering of the merely human. Such is the curious dialectic of liberty.

This should not really surprise us. The supposedly humanistic philosophies always cut man down to size, made him something trivial and enslaved. Freud cut him down to a bundle of complexes, enslaved by his childhood traumas; Marx cut him down to a merely economic being, enslaved by the dialectic of history; popular Darwinism cut him down to a specialised mammal and no more. One might add that in most oriental religious systems, the life of the individual is more or less unreal or unimportant.

It is only in the old Western tradition, and above all in Catholic Christianity, that man becomes something great. He needs to be personally humble. But he also needs to remember, and to enact, the principle that he is an immortal being, made in the image and likeness of God and bought with the full price of God's blood, a citizen of no mean city, having a destiny of more than royal splendour. By giving a certain formal and courteous and ceremonial character to the routines of daily life, he both asserts this principle and strengthens his own apprehension of it. (One supreme instance of this is provided by the slow austere dignity of life in a good Benedictine abbey, such as that of Fontgombault, near Poitiers in France. From a recent visit there, I carried away an extraordinarily powerful impression of the greatness of man, as asserted and enacted by this community of men concerned solely with the greatness of God. The paradox is only apparent.)

In today's world, Ceremony seems to be in retreat everywhere. Even in the worship of God, even in some monasteries, her reign is under attack. But she still retains a good deal of influence there, and also in the law courts, and in armies, and in the public acts of government: there are still certain occasions upon which men desire to enact a lofty image of themselves.

Traditionally, she was one of the presiding deities of a university. Even in my own days at Oxford, student life retained certain ritual or ceremonial elements. The scholar's cap and gown—stylized versions of the priest's cassock and biretta—were worn habitually: the daily dinner in Hall was a stately affair, with the undergraduates rising to their feet as the gowned Fellows filed in, and with a Latin grace then recited under the severe gaze of those long-dead College notabilities whose portraits lined the ancient stone walls. And these things did not have the self-consciousness of an act put on: they were the natural and inherited pattern of academic life, reaching their climax in the quasiliturgical ceremony by which we were made into Bachelors or Masters *in nomine Domini*. And so—whatever the nature of our specialized studies, whatever the foolishness of our private selves—we paid tribute to the dignity of learning, the greatness of our inheritance.

Were I in command of things, I would give Ceremony a considerable re-enthronement in every university and college. I would attach particular importance to that formal dinner in Hall. It is a serious thing, a quasi-sacramental thing to eat in common with a measure of ritual: it is an assertion and enactment of collegiate identity, of corporate life, of the academic family, and it is of great educational and civilizing potency. Let the Hall be like the chapel and the library, a serious and beautiful place, with Ceremony gently presiding: something ugly and barbarising is said, something untrue as well, when the act of eating is reduced to a sprawled and casual consumption of nutrition-units, hastily grabbed in some functional cafeteria.

Perhaps personal nostalgia is here causing me to ask too much. Ceremony costs money, and is not always acceptable even to the best of young people: nor can instant antiquity be purchased by those who now establish colleges.

Even so, the underlying principle deserves some observance; and I find this in the courteous and decent behaviour of these students. They prove that one can indeed refrain from being a slob or a slattern or a lout: on some campuses that I have known, the possibility has seemed to be very much in doubt.

They also suggest various further reflections upon the nature and content and method of an education that will deserve to be called 'liberal'. I am thinking here of the last stage of one's general education, of the process by which one is helped to maturity as a human being and a free one: I have little to say about the high-school education of adolescents, and nothing about the later and more specialized studies which make one into a doctor or a lawyer or a historian.

Such a liberal education must of course presuppose some kind of good general schooling; and here, I would want to lay emphasis upon two things.

In the first place, the student who embarks upon a liberal education at the college level should already possess a certain ability to think and a good command of his own language. This might seem a very obvious and unexacting requirement. But certain supposedly 'progressive' tendencies in present-day education — on both sides of the Atlantic—have made it an embarrassingly high requirement in fact: the sceptical philosophies already mentioned, together with a feeling that the pursuit of excellence is elitist and undemocratic and that the schoolchild must be allowed to 'do his own thing', have created a situation in which many a high-school graduate has an extremely poor vocabulary and hardly any ability to use his mind and his language accurately. For most practical purposes, he comes close to being inarticulate and illiterate.

He is then the victim of a wider phenomenon, at which I hinted in an earlier chapter. People often say that ours is a corrupt society, a dying culture: they commonly turn out to be thinking chiefly of sex and drugs. I would place greater emphasis upon the corruption of language and the intellect. The dominant philosophies of the day are such as to deny and ultimately destroy the intellect, unless they are treated strictly as a game: associated with these but distinct from them, there prevails in our time a clear retreat from language as such, a linguistic corruption which (as George Orwell observed) has a close and causal relationship with political and social corruption. If an Englishman may be allowed to say so, a perfect example was provided by the linguistic habits of the Nixon White House: our own public life provides many examples which are hardly less perfect.

I suggest two remedies at the high-school level, ancient and rather unfashionable but well-tried and effective. As a first training in the accurate use of the mind, I recommend Euclidean geometry to begin with, and the rudiments of formal logic to follow. And while a good command of language can be acquired by much talking and listening, by much reading and writing, it is helped along wonderfully by the intensive study of Latin. There is no better way of causing a schoolboy to attend to the *exact* meaning of a word or a sentence: there is no better education in the difference between saying what you mean and uttering vague sounds which more or less suggest the sort of thing you have in mind. The study of any foreign or ancient language will have this effect in some measure, especially if it is a highly-inflected language, structurally unlike English: the best second choice might well be Russian, and this language will introduce the student to a great literature. But the study of Latin will introduce him to a greater literature, of closer relevance to his inheritance as a Western man and a Christian; and as a mind-sharpener, it is without rival.

Let the student approach his liberal education at college, therefore, with at least an initial facility in the use of language and thought. The college will develop this: it should not need to start at the beginning.

But there is a second preliminary requirement, one which needs rather careful statement. The free man's great danger and temptation is pride: he may come to admire himself and despise the slave. And a corresponding danger goes along with any fully liberal education such as I have been considering. This must be (among other things) a liberation from scepticism: it must be an education in answers, not merely in questions. But it is a distinctly dangerous thing to tell a clever young man that he now knows the answers, especially if he is at all conceited by nature: all too probably, he will become an arrogant prig.

Spiritually and psychologically, it is certainly a dangerous thing to be right and to know you're right. Some people are so acutely aware of this danger that they want us to admit uncertainty at every point, offering no more than a tentative opinion about anything. But this is to evade the problem, not to solve it: we might then find personal humility easier to maintain, but only at the cost of sterilising the whole intellectual process and chaining ourselves up again in the prison of scepticism.

The right answer, surely, is to be so formed—spiritually and psychologically—that one can reach certainty and cherish it and proclaim it without falling into intellectual pride. This is, in the first instance, a religious and moral problem, the individual's responsibility, the concern also of parents and pastors. But it is the concern of education as well, and at all levels. This will convey certainty, in the Faith and in much else. But explicitly and by steady implication, it will also offer constant reminders that while reality can be known, it cannot be known completely and must always remain mysterious. It will not offer knowledge as any kind of swaggering proprietorship over reality: its essentially religious character means that it will encourage the student to look upon the Creator and His works in a habitual spirit of awe and reverence and humility, and to act with a corresponding gentleness and restraint.

If this is to happen in fact, the student's prior formation will need to be of the heart, not only of the soul and the intellect: he must be habitually open to large and generous responses of the emotions and the imagination. He is to inherit the freedom of the mind, and he must prepare himself by deserving this, by discarding that servile mentality which—in an earlier chapter—I exemplified in the fictional characters of 'Hooper' and 'Mark Studdock'. This is the school's task, the home's as well; and it is to be mostly achieved by those cultural interests and activities to which—at one time—the name of 'Poetry' was given, though in a much wider sense than that word bears today.

As a literary man, I'd lay much emphasis here upon 'poetry' in the modern and narrower sense; but I'd want it to be assimilated and enjoyed and absorbed into the mind, rather than being laid out on the dissecting-table. Let it be chanted appreciatively in chorus, memorable prose as well: let it sink into the mind. It's better to know twenty good poems by heart than merely to have read two hundred: it's better to sing, or to play some instrument even badly, than to listen to the radio. Let there be much solitary reading: let the easy tears of adolescence be shed freely over all the heroic myths and legends and tragedies in the world. And let there be some formation in courtesy—chiefly that formation which comes from living among courteous people, but also the kind that comes from instruction in good handwriting or formal dancing, in all the arts and rituals of civilised living.

Such things naturally don't add up to the full content of a high-school education: they are offered as a rough indication of the respects in which too many young people, although technically qualified for a liberal arts college, are imperfectly prepared for the freedom which it should give them. It's a great thing to apprehend the truth. But before that, one needs to be the kind of person to whom the truth can safely be entrusted. The liberated slave who retains an essential servility of the mind is going to dishonour the name of freedom.

Being thus qualified to receive the liberation of truth worthily, the student approaches the college and asks it to give him the relevant sort of education. What form will this take? What will be its pattern?

The main thing (I suggest) is that it will *have* a pattern: it will recognise that there is a natural hierarchy or sequence of disciplines, and in particular, that the philosophical and theological problem is logically anterior to every other kind of educational problem. It needs to be settled first. If there is no God, then every kind of religious education is radically misleading: if there is a God, then every kind of education which is not primarily centred around that fact is going to guide the students into a dream-world. And it is not possible to prescind from this dilemma, even if we so desire. A college which simply puts the whole question of religion to one side is going to teach its students that religion is something that can be put to one side; and all the more effectively, since that dogma will be taken for granted rather than being stated. The primary questions come first: until we've answered them, we can't hope to make much sense of the secondary questions.

To speak like this is, of course, to challenge the modern democratic sentiment which desires all subjects or disciplines to exist side by side, on equal terms as it were, like the commodities on the shelves of some supermarket. There they are, in fraternal equality: 'Philosophy', 'Religion', 'Education'; 'Latin', 'Greek', 'Mathematics'; 'Art', 'Beauticraft', 'Chinese', each as good as its neighbour. You can major in any of these or in a great many others, you can take your doctorate in any of them and become a great expert. And since one can't do all things in a single lifetime, the effort of achieving expertise in any one of them means that you'll give very little attention to the others.

The present-day university scene, European and American, is dominated by this concept, which might be called 'The Democratic Autonomy and Equality of Subjects'. It makes practical sense in a way: that is, there cannot be great achievement in any field without a high degree of specialisation. But unless very heavily qualified, it is an illusory principle: it is based upon a studied or sceptical ignoring of the fact that there *is* a natural hierarchy or sequence of disciplines, that there *are* primary and secondary questions. The failure to recognise this is a prime reason for today's breakdown of liberal education.

It can be detected in respect of all fields; but I think it becomes most clearly visible in the social sciences. In my country, you can go straight from school and embark upon a full-time degree course in (say) Sociology. This is, perhaps, a real discipline. But it is a discipline which at every stage presupposes some notion of what human beings are, of what their life should be, of what they are *for*. And these are subjects about which different opinions are in fact held. If sociological enquiry starts from the premise that Christianity is true, it takes one kind of pattern: if it starts from the premise that Marxism is true, it takes a sharply different kind of pattern. Either pattern could be justified, according to your belief in Jesus or in Karl. What can not be justified, however, is a situation in which that prior question is bundled out of sight or taken for granted. It needs to be faced: it needs to be settled first.

What happens in fact is that cheerful boys, football-loving and girl-loving, go straight from school and sit at the feet of their sociology lecturers, totally unaware of the unexamined philosophical and theological (or atheological) presuppositions which lie behind what the lecturer is saying. Unexamined by the lecturer, probably: he's a sociologist, he has no time for philosophy or theology. Unexamined by those cheerful students, almost certainly.

If only the product were properly labelled! One might imagine an ideal university in which one course was marked 'This is what sociology looks like if you start from Marxist premises', and another 'This is what sociology looks like if you start from Christian premises'. And if some bewildered student were to ask very sensibly 'But which premises are true—the Marxist ones, or the Christian ones?', he would be referred back to a logically anterior course, philosophical and theological in scope.

He should have gone through that course earlier. It makes no kind of sense to study the secondary questions until you've fought your way through the primary questions. If you try to do so, it will be a brain-washing that you get, rather than an education; and you won't even know that it's happening.

A good liberal education will therefore take questions in due order: it will establish sound first principles, and will then go on to particulars. But the structure appropriate to it can also be considered from another angle, less philosophical and more pedagogical.

According to an old joke, basic education consists of the three Rs: Reading, Riting, and Rithmetic. One learns the rudiments of those three things at school. But one prime task of the liberal arts college is to take them further—to press all three forward, with full intellectual rigour, right up to the limit of the student's capacity. He can already use language and the mind after a fashion: he must now learn to use them as precision instruments. The college must therefore teach three initial arts: the art of Grammar, which can be crudely described as 'how to read'; the art of Rhetoric, which can be crudely described as 'how to write and speak'; and the art of Logic, which can be rather less crudely described as 'how to think'. Thereafter (though perhaps with less urgency) it needs to concern itself with numbers, with mathematics—not for the essentially servile purposes of the counting-house and the computer-room, but for the religious and liberal purpose of perceiving the order and beauty of God's creation in another mode than that of language. Hence it will teach such purely mathematical disciplines as Arithmetic and Geometry, applying them afterwards to such lovely fields as Music and Astronomy. (These can and should be included in the subject-matter of aesthetic and cultural education as well. But under that aspect, they fall within the preliminary field of 'Poetry' and are the school's business rather than the college's— which is not to say that an aesthetic concern with them should terminate with one's schooldays. It would be a sad thing if the student came to understand the mathematical theory of music while ceasing to enjoy it: it would be an equally sad thing if he worked his way through Ptolemy to Einstein and forgot how loudly and splendidly the night sky proclaims the glory of God.)

It will be observed that this particular marshalling of subjects corresponds with the old sevenfold way of the Liberal Arts, the *Trivium* of three verbal arts and the *Quadrivium* of four numerate arts. In recommending this pattern for present-day liberal education, I may be suspected of romantic mediaevalism, of some kind of hostility to more recent developments. Let me therefore say that I do believe in the progress of knowledge—and also, in the principle that if knowledge is to develop, it can only do so by building upon secure foundations previously established. (No building will rise to any great height if we make it our daily concern to demolish what we added to it yesterday.)

The Middle Ages didn't know everything: in a whole host of matters, a schoolboy of today knows things of which the greatest philosophers of that time had no inkling. (He is also open and vulnerable to fallacies which the most amateurish philosophers of that time would have avoided easily: so are too many of his teachers.) But it seems clear that in the Seven Liberal Arts, our forefathers worked out a basic intellectual structure of immense practical durability. Scientific and other developments, inconceivable to them, can be fitted into it without stress and so take their place within the hierarchy of knowledge: within any other framework that I know or can imagine, they would be unrelated particulars, lying meaninglessly side by side like the competitive packages in some supermarket.

One cannot be taught everything in a four-year liberal arts course. But the student can at least ask the college to give him a mental framework, a set of criteria by which ideas can be judged and a structure into which they can be fitted if they so deserve.

The Seven Liberal Arts, when fortified by the supervisory presence of the Catholic Faith, provide just such a framework and structure—one which has stood the test of time, and has not in the faintest degree been proved invalid by the countless discoveries which have been made since it was first formulated. In no pedantic or archaicising spirit, a good liberal arts college will make this its foundation.

Upon that foundation, it will erect a temple of wide reading. No, it will not encourage a study of the Great Books: it will be concerned with the apprehension of reality, and with the use of the Great Books as means to that end. It will thus pay to each of the great thinkers and writers, to Plato and Marx and Freud and Maritain equally, a compliment which they don't always get in the universities. They tried to direct our attention to something other than themselves and their writings: too frequently, the students and scholars of this age frustrate that attempt, looking not at what the man is saying, but at him and at the fact that he's saying it. Even the lousiest thinker deserves more politeness than that: we owe him him the elementary courtesy of paying attention to what he's saying, and then judging it (perhaps adversely) on its merits.

A good liberal arts college will therefore concentrate upon original texts rather than upon commentaries, and will look *through* them rather than *at* them. It is perhaps debatable how far this policy should be pressed. A free and educated man certainly needs to know something about Marxism: it is not so clear that he needs to have suffered his way through every last boring page of *Das Kapital*. There is room here for a certain give-and-take.

But the basic principle is clear. The object of a liberal education is reality or truth, not the different things that men have thought and said about reality and truth, useful though these will be as aids to thought. The 'history of thought' has a secondary kind of importance: it is one of those specialised disciplines which are properly studied at the later postgraduate level. But it does have a qualified relevance to liberal education. Taken wrongly, it can become an indoctrination in sceptical relativism: this man said this, that man said that, who knows? But the student who reads the Great Books—many of them written in societies and cultures quite unlike his own—is going to misunderstand them at many points, and seriously, if he doesn't know something of the background against which each was written, the lines along which men were thinking at the time, the ideas which they unconsciously took for granted, the arguments in which they were engaged. Bring to the *Symposium*—or, for that matter, to *Genesis*—the mental 'set' which you picked up as a high-school student in London or Kansas City, and you'll get a confused notion of what's being talked about. You'll need some degree of background explanation and help.

With various such qualifications, let us dream of an education which studies reality with the help provided by the great books, within the sound load-bearing structure provided by the Seven Liberal Arts and in the light of the Catholic Faith. Let us not talk of options and specialisations until later: our field is the broad structure of reality in general, with every student and every teacher engaged with all parts of it. Let the classes be small and informal, tutorials or seminars rather than lectures: let there be no class-war of students *vs.* faculty and administration, but only a brotherhood or community of seekers and finders. And let the seeking and finding be timeless, democratic: let Plato and Aquinas and Descartes and Freud come among us as equals—they are only men, after all, just like ourselves—giving what they can give, submitting like you and me to the common judgment of faith and reason, consenting to be wrong where they are proved wrong, happy to be right where they turn out to be right, and all contributing to our greater knowledge of that which it is is a free man's duty and destiny to know, of God, in Himself and in His Creation.

But dreams are dreams. Could such an education *work*?

I'm glad you picked on this moment to ask me that question. A year ago, I might have given it a rather negative answer.

Chapter IX:
DREAM AND REALITY

For the most part, this book has been an attempt to analyse my own strongly positive response to the experience of visiting one small and newly established institution. For a long time previously, I had cherished various dreams and hunches about what liberal education ought to be, for some fortunate students if not for all: this experience confirmed those dreams and hunches in certain respects while supplementing and correcting them in others.

It did something else, of possibly greater importance: it provided me with the hardest kind of empirical evidence that liberal education—as so conceived—does actually work.

It was for this reason that I decided to offer this book to the public. The appeal or interest of its theme might be considered extremely narrow. A single small institution is plainly going to be of direct practical interest to a limited number of people only: my own responses to it concern nobody but myself. A guest should always send his appreciative thank-you letter afterwards; but this will seldom have the length of even a short book, and can very seldom be expected to interest third parties.

On the other hand, we all need to know what can be done in the field of education and what can not: this is a matter of wide public concern. And it seems to me likely that if I—or anyone else—were to set forth a pure vision or dream of what an ideal liberal education should be, on the lines indicated in these pages, the general response would be sceptical. "Yes, yes; that is indeed a pretty vision of yours. But it's no more than a vision. It couldn't be made to work. You'd never assemble a faculty with the singleness of purpose that you have in mind; you'd never find students who'd submit to the rigorous intellectual discipline that you propose; and you'd never find parents who'd be willing to pay for their sons and daughters to receive so unpractical an education on such very untried and experimental lines."

Such doubts make obvious sense: until recently, I'd have expressed them myself, recognising the fantasy-element in those dreams and fancies of my own. Even now, I would not suggest that those three difficulties are unreal or unimportant. The imaginary critic whom I have just quoted has a strong case. His last point, of course, is only valid in a limited and relative way: the concept and method here proposed is just about the best-tried and most clearly successful thing in educational history. But many parents will be unaware of this, and will see it as a mere eccentric innovation; and it does in fact have a certain untried and experimental character so far as its application to modern circumstances and modern people is concerned.

The difficulties are real and indeed obvious. But the fact that they can be overcome in practice, that the dream does work and is working at this moment, is — I suggest — of very considerable public importance.

It has a distinctive importance at this time, since so many alternative kinds of education are manifestly *not* working. As I observed at an early point, present-day societies—Western and Communist too—are able to train any number of first-class doctors and engineers and so forth: so far as education is concerned with the imparting of those exacting applied skills which I have unkindly called 'servile', it is in good shape. But liberal education—in *any* sense of that expression—is in very bad shape. It has been observed in many countries that it is producing a generation of near-illiterates, thus failing in the most elementary task of all; and the present condition of the fine arts—notably, the fact that pop-and-rock music is the overwhelmingly dominant artform of this age, with erotic self-pity as its dominant theme—suggests to me that in its further and cultural role, liberal education is fighting a losing battle, if indeed it is fighting at all.

The clearest evidence, perhaps, is provided by the fact of student alienation. This gets into the news from time to time, but only when it reaches the point of more or less violent expression, as happened in the United States during the 1960s and happens fairly regularly in France. In the motivation of such violence, there are obvious political elements. But those political passions flourish in the soil of a more general discontent: throughout today's West, it is common form for the student to see the 'liberal' side of his education in cynical or bitter terms. At the best, he will often see it as an introduction to agreeable pastimes: too often, he will see it as an arbitrary and meaningless ritual which has to be gone through so that he can graduate and thus qualify for a good status and salary. Seldom indeed will he see it as an acquisition of wisdom.

His consequent disillusionment and alienation is the inevitable consequence of the fundamental scepticism which prevails in adult society. Clever about the 'servile' means, we of the older generation are hopelessly divided and uncertain about those ends or ultimates which are the proper concern of the free man, and it follows that there is a central falsity in any claim that we make to offer a liberal education. But we continue to make the claim, hoping that the mere educational process in itself—regardless of its content or its ultimate lack of content—will somehow make up for our own deficiency, our own poverty.

It doesn't. Nobody can give what he hasn't got; and in general, the older generation today simply doesn't possess what the younger generation is rightly seeking. Nor does the great god Education possess any magical power that will remedy this situation.

The power of some greater God will need to be invoked; and I have already made it clear that in my own view, the Catholic Faith is the answer to the scepticism of the day and therefore to our educational problem at its deepest level.

I would therefore like to be able to report that although liberal education generally is in bad shape, Catholic liberal education is thriving and confident. But unfortunately, this is not what we find.

I do not want to dwell on the negative side of my subject, and I am certainly not going to say unkind things about named people and institutions. Nor do I want my present fortuitous concentration upon the American scene to suggest any kind of anti-American purpose: the trouble exists in many countries or most. But it needs to be said in all charity that in the United States today, the typical Catholic liberal arts college is in very bad shape indeed, the typical Catholic university too.

This is primarily because of the tendency already mentioned, the current weakening and distortion of faith among the Catholic intelligentsia. Because of this tendency, it has become the normal thing—not exceptional at all—for the supposed Catholicism of many colleges and universities to be something quite different in reality. The outlook or philosophy now dominant, assiduously preached by most of the faculty and eagerly embraced by most of the students, will indeed contain certain elements or memories of Catholicism. But it contains much more powerful elements of modernism, of scepticism, of evolutionary relativism, of existentialism, of Marxism, of many another -ism which has become fashionable in the non-Catholic world. In so far as it continues to be religious at all, the religion in question is commonly a kind of free-for-all syncretism, 'humanitarian' on lines which actually promote totalitarian cruelty, Gnostic in so far as it is spiritually-minded at all, and wholly compatible with each individual's total freedom to follow his own fancy in every matter of faith and morals and worship. And the freedom in question is unreal: in practice, it is the enslaving bewilderment of the uninformed shopper who finds himself in a notably chaotic supermarket—a supermarket, moreover, in which very few of the foods on sale are either appetising or nourishing. They are attractively packaged, and are promoted deafeningly. But most of them are bad for you, and some are poisonous.

There are individuals who hold out gallantly, institutions too: I am not suggesting that this particular college is wholly unique. But the overall picture is as I have said. Within American higher education today, it is becoming increasingly unreal to apply the adjective 'Catholic' to institutions which once claimed it proudly and with good reason. In a number of cases, the college has frankly renounced its claim to have a distinctively Catholic character, usually in return for government money. This was at least honest. But that claim often continues to be made, even where it has lost all plausibility.

In this situation, the future of the 'Catholic' college is plainly limited. It was always a somewhat expensive option, as compared with—say—the state university. Parents paid that extra money, and willingly, so that their sons and daughters could be educated in a Catholic atmosphere and on Catholic principles. But where that atmosphere has been dissipated and those principles abandoned, there is no reason why they should continue to do so. There is, in fact, ample reason why they should cease to do so if they wish their children to retain the Faith; and this is slowly dawning upon many of them, with obvious financial consequences for the colleges.

A movement or tendency which was supposed to breathe new life into Catholic higher education shows every sign of breathing death into it.

So far, I have been talking about the American version of a world-wide tendency. The crisis of faith is not confined to the United States, nor are its consequences for Catholic higher education, and the situation just described could be paralleled in many other countries or most, though with sharp national or regional differences.

None the less, there are certain distinctively American elements in this situation, without close parallel elsewhere.

As a foreigner, I must speak carefully here. But it seems to me clear that Catholic higher education in the United States—a colossal achievement in its day, and one that seemed until recently to have the most solid and enduring character—had from the start a fatal weakness, by reason of the situation faced by the Catholic community in America. Ever since the nineteenth century, American Catholics in general have been under considerable pressure to conform, at least outwardly, to the dominant values of their society. It was a society chiefly Protestant and already somewhat prosperous, and many of them came to it as poor immigrants, ethnically distinct and therefore held in low esteem by some people, and distinctly suspect as regards their loyalty to the United States. As Roman Catholics, did they not owe their ultimate allegiance to a foreign potentate, the Bishop of Rome? Were they not obliged to make important mental reservations when they went through the process of naturalisation, and whenever they recited the Pledge of Allegiance thereafter? Americans now and proud of it, they resented all such suspicions—perhaps with an uneasy background awareness that a real question does arise at this point and always must; and so, not only for self-protection, they made great efforts to prove themselves one-hundred-and-one-per-cent Americans, to fly the flag more bravely than others, to recite the Pledge of Allegiance more proudly.

Their psychology, and some aspects of their behaviour, thus came to differ sharply from that of their co-religionists in England. In his bones, every English Catholic remembers the long centuries of persecution: his immediate folk-heroes—More, Fisher, Campion, and the rest—are men who died (technically speaking) as traitors to their country: in its spirit and in its particular institutions, his educational system is that of an underground or a resistance movement. His faults and follies can be as great as anybody's; but it never occurs to him to identify unreservedly with 'the world' as he meets it, with the secular order of his own country. This sense of being a separate people, a kind of opposition, is perhaps weakening today; but its weakening displays a close correlation with the English version of that general weakening of faith which I have mentioned earlier. The English Catholic, if he's strong in the Faith, looks with distrust and detachment upon the world about him. He has no particular confidence in the British government: it killed too many of his Catholic forebears for that, and if it now does something blatantly wicked—such as legitimising abortion—he is distressed but he isn't in the least 'shocked' in the sense of being surprised.

For good or for ill—for good *and* for ill, I'd say—his American counterpart is still in the converse situation. I travel very widely in the United States, and I find everywhere a very high correlation between strength in the Faith and patriotic confidence in the secular order of the country. One consequence of this was the shock, the surprise, the trauma inflicted upon good Catholics by the Supreme Court decision which authorised abortion. It wasn't just the sad ugly fact of sin, to which all Christians are accustomed: what upset them was the spectacle of gross wickedness being formally endorsed with all due process under the Constitution, which they had supposed themselves able to trust without reserve.

This point and contrast could be developed. Its relevance for our present subject lies in the fact that American Catholics were strongly motivated to conform; to be exactly like other Americans, with their unpopular religion withdrawn into private life and private observance; to make their higher education just like any other kind of higher education, but with the Faith simply added. In the system that so developed, theology and Catholic philosophy could of course be taught, and were in fact taught admirably, and were rightly given a role of the supervisory, sapiential, or magisterial kind. But seldom indeed were they seen as the basis upon which the *whole* of liberal education was to be built. They were packaged up with it, they were expected to influence it. But they were nearly always seen as something distinct from it.

A split-mindedness resulted, of the kind which I have mentioned in an earlier chapter; and this was both intellectual and (if this is the right word) ideological. The college taught the Catholic Faith with one hand (so to speak), while with the other, it educated people by means of ideas and texts and methods which had been developed elsewhere, on markedly non-Catholic assumptions, and were intellectually in conflict with the Faith at countless points. And in the same way, it assumed that the ideology of secular liberal education—its values and purposes and orientations—could be taken over and made to play just the same part in a Catholic liberal education, given only a vaguely supervisory presence of the Church and the Faith. Before the class and after it, a prayer would indeed be said, and this was all to the good. But it was taken for granted that in many fields or most, the class itself could be just the same as it would be if there were no prayers anywhere and no God at all.

In effect, the Catholic college tried to make itself acceptable by playing the world's educational game on very much the world's own terms, with 'religion' adding a corrective touch here and there, but mostly remaining in the background as a private and personal extra, not related very closely to education as such. Seldom indeed was any attempt made to devise an education that would start with the Faith, and end with it, and be governed and judged by it at every point, in the physics laboratory no less than in the theology classroom. Any such attempt would have been an explicit challenge to 'the world', and (in practice) to 'the American world'; and any such challenge would have been psychologically difficult to make, since it would have seemed vaguely unpatriotic, vaguely un-American, and the Catholic community was strongly motivated to give no impression of that kind.

Now I do not share the view of those who regard the American version of 'the world' as outstandingly evil, deserving a more-than-Calvinistic denunciation at every point. (This is a view which now finds lavish expression on many a post-Catholic campus: people tend to rush from one extreme to the other.) Nor do I want the big transatlantic difference just mentioned to be interpreted as implying greater wisdom on our side: Catholic higher education in England has certainly avoided the mistake and split-mindedness which I am talking about, but it has done so by the simple method of not existing at all.

But if Catholic Christianity is to be taken seriously, it necessarily involves a radical break with 'the world', a radical challenge to 'the world', in whatever form this may locally present itself; and this necessity has its serious consequences for education.

A certain reluctance to face it squarely caused much of Catholic higher education in America to weaken itself most imprudently by playing a double game—as though in this particular field, it was somehow possible to remain with Christ and yet go along (for the most part) with those who were squarely against Him. So weakened, so divided in heart and head, it was in no state to face the exceptional stresses of the 1960s and the early 1970s. To a huge extent and by every relevant standard, it therefore ceased—during this recent period—to work.

It became like a mass of dead leaves, such as you might see in the spring, the grey mouldering remains of last year's Fall. But within the Church, the Founder's pattern of death and resurrection is constantly being re-enacted; and here and there, if you look closely at that grey heap, you can see a tiny green shoot.

If Christ is indeed the great and only Liberator, if the world without Him is indeed a prison and a slavery, it follows that any real liberal education must be ordered *at every point* towards Him and governed *at every point* by the Faith of His Church. Necessarily, then, it will offer an explicit challenge to the world in all its versions, and to the academic and intellectual world in particular. It will recognise the excellent work done in many fields by non-Catholic and even by atheistic thinkers, and will make full use of this. But it will do so cautiously: all such work will be under judgment, will incur an initial degree of distrust which will often be dissipated before long. And it will continually remember and assert that its purpose is radically different—not just marginally different—from that of liberal education elsewhere. In either case, the desired end-product can be defined as the free man, the educated *liberalis*. But the meaning of any such expression differs sharply, according to whether you accept or reject the Catholic notion of the slavery or thraldom into which men are born and of the freedom into which (under grace) the truth can lead them.

The matter can therefore be stated very simply indeed. A genuinely liberal education will be one based upon the objective and final truth of the Catholic Faith, and upon an uncompromising application of that Faith to every question that arises within the educational process.

It is my task, my purpose in this book to bear witness to the fact that a liberal education, when so conceived, does in fact liberate—and not only in the spiritual and otherworldly sense which matters most of all, but also in any number of immediate, personal, and human senses. It works.

In particular, it generates happiness; and I would like to end as I began, on that note. If I were a great theologian or philosopher, or even a very good man, I would doubtlessly start and finish on some higher note. But if God is indeed our Father, then parental considerations must have their importance and dignity; and it was with a father's anxiety that I approached this whole question, being intensely aware of the alienation and stress which so many young people suffer nowadays, and the tendency of college education to heighten this rather than to ease it. All kinds of good work are still being done in all kinds of institutions, and the resilence of youth means that stress is often less disastrous than seemed likely at first: Oxford remains a pleasant and rewarding place for study, and I have found both laughter and wisdom on many an American campus. It remains true, however, that a profound malaise and disorientation afflicts most liberal education in the present-day West, and that while society at large is impoverished thereby, the young people are the first to suffer.

Here, at this college which I must leave tomorrow with much regret—and not without saying a fond good-bye to those ducks on the lake—the young people are spared that kind of suffering. Their life is not exactly easy: very hard work is expected of them, and much of it is highly abstract and otherwise difficult. But they apply themselves to it with dedication and in high spirits, as prisoners might when tunneling their laborious way to freedom.

They represent a great hope for the future, an example which ought to be followed widely; and if I may say so, they carry a message of particular importance for a nation whose most sacred text speaks of happiness as something which can be *pursued*.

There's another sacred text which says "Seek first the Kingdom".

Ordering information for this book will be found under the copyright notice.